Y0-DBS-627

WHAT TO DO
WHEN YOUR
BILLS
EXCEED YOUR
PAYCHECK

WHAT TO DO WHEN YOUR BILLS EXCEED YOUR PAYCHECK

Sidney Sherwin, ATTORNEY AT LAW
Member, New York Bar and Federal Bar

PRENTICE-HALL, INC.
Englewood Cliffs, New Jersey

What to Do When Your Bills Exceed Your Paycheck, by Sidney Sherwin
Copyright © 1974 by Sidney Sherwin
All rights reserved. No part of this book may be
reproduced in any form or by any means, except
for the inclusion of brief quotations in a review,
without permission in writing from the publisher.
Printed in the United States of America
Prentice-Hall International, Inc., London
Prentice-Hall of Australia, Pty. Ltd., Sydney
Prentice-Hall of Canada, Ltd., Toronto
Prentice-Hall of India Private Ltd., New Delhi
Prentice-Hall of Japan, Inc., Tokyo

10 9 8 7 6 5 4 3 2 1

Library of Congress Cataloging in Publication Data

Sherwin, Sidney.
   What to do when your bills exceed your paycheck.

   1. Debtor and creditor—United States—Popular
works. I. Title.
KF1501.Z9S53   346'.73'077   74–1396
ISBN 0–13–955039–9
ISBN 0–13–955021–6 (pbk.)

To my partner, my best friend—my wife, Zecie

Introduction

The time that it will take you to read this book may save you many months of worry or help you avoid unnecessary or even dangerous actions in connection with your debts. Moreover, the time you spend with this book should also prevent you from getting deeper into debt.

Many of the legal forms used throughout the book are based upon actual cases; the names, however, have been changed. The purpose of showing legal forms is to give the layman a better understanding of the situations discussed within the text. *But these legal forms should only be used by attorneys, or with the advice of an attorney.* In some instances they legally may be used without an attorney, but to do so would be analogous to a layman's trying to take out his own bad tooth.

Most references to laws concern the statutes and "common law" of the state of New York. The reason for this is that the writer is a practicing New York attorney. However, the basic principles discussed apply almost universally throughout our 50 states. But if you contemplate any legal action in connection with your debts as a result of reading this book, it is *essential*—for your own protection—that you consult an attorney.

Remember, too, that a real estate broker or a notary public is not an attorney, and his advice should not be sought in legal matters.

Contents

This book is not intended to give legal advice. Rather, its purpose is to acquaint you generally with the areas of law discussed, and the problems you may be faced with in your relationship to your creditors and alleged creditors. If you feel that you need legal advice, you should consult a lawyer, and do so as quickly as possible.

one

Facts Everyone Needs to Know

BEFORE YOU SIGN

Everyone should remember the following rules of thumb before signing any contract:

(a) Read the contract very carefully and make sure you understand everything it says. If you don't understand any word or words in the contract, strike out those words and let the salesman put the writing in terms you understand. Remember, just because you are given a piece of paper with writing on it does not mean you must accept automatically everything it contains. You have the right to negotiate to make any changes that you wish made in the contract.

If the seller doesn't want to make changes, and you do not want to buy without having them made, nobody is forcing you to sign this contract. Perhaps you can buy the product or service involved elsewhere, with the changes that you desire made in writing.

(b) Don't sign anything you don't understand; consult an attorney if the amount involved is substantial. Once the contract is signed it may be too late for an attorney to help you.

(c) Don't sign any incomplete contract; you may be met with surprises later on. If for some valid reason you do sign a contract that is not fully completed, make sure you get a copy. In fact, it's a good idea to get a copy of any contract you sign.

(d) Don't rely on the word of any salesman, no matter how sincere or honest he may seem to you. "Sales-puff" is not part of a contract, and it cannot be a warranty or guarantee. If the salesman promises you anything that you want to rely on, make him put it into writing in the contract.

(e) Understand the arithmetic of any contract you sign. Know exactly how much you are paying for the article or service and how much of the price is for interest or "service charges."

Congress recently passed a "Truth in Lending" law. This law requires merchants and finance companies to show the *exact cost* of the article purchased on an installment plan, including the total amount of interest and service charges, as well as the yearly interest rate charged. However, legal rates of interest vary in each state. You may refer to the interest rate chart in Exhibit 1 of the Appendix to determine the current legal rate of interest allowed in your state. You may then compute the interest from a rate table obtained at your local bank or library.

The Truth in Lending Law will be discussed further in a later chapter, along with other means of consumer protection provided by the Federal, state, and local governments.

(f) Do not give any deposit before you get a receipt explaining exactly why the deposit was given.

(g) If you become ill or some accident prevents you from paying your debts, inform or have someone else inform your creditor. Creditors are human; something can be worked out.

IF YOU ARE BROUGHT TO COURT

Before a creditor can collect any money, he must first obtain a judgment. A judgment is a decision of the court that the creditor is legally entitled to the benefits he seeks. Only after a judgment is obtained in the courts can the creditor "execute" upon your property or obtain "an income execution" (formerly known as a garnishee) on your salary.

There are instances where a creditor may bring an action in court and recover a judgment against you after repossessing the merchandise you bought. This judgment is known as a "deficiency judgment." Ostensibly, this means that the creditor has taken back the goods he sold to you pursuant to his retail installment contract, note, or security agreement, and that upon selling those goods at a public or private sale, insufficient funds were received to pay the amount of money you were obligated to pay. Therefore, there is a deficiency or balance due, for which he sued and obtained a judgment.

Before a creditor can obtain a judgment he must naturally begin a lawsuit. All lawsuits are commenced by serving a summons. On the summons itself, or on a separate sheet, a complaint, or statement of the creditor's claim, is also served upon the defendant.

When served with a summons, many debtors foolishly believe they can simply ignore it, especially if they think they do not owe any money. That is not true. A summons must be answered, because failure to do so will result in a default judgment. In fact, many creditors make their summonses appear to be folded circulars of no importance in the hope that their debtors will ignore the summons so that they can obtain a judgment by default.

For his own sake, a debtor must answer a summons. By "answer" we mean advise the court of your defense to this suit in accordance with the demands of the summons, or turn the summons over to an attorney who will answer for you. If you cannot afford an attorney, you can go directly to the court whose address is listed in the summons and tell your defense to the clerk of the court.

A recent study by the New York Regional Consumer Protective Council found that to a large extent default judgments were entered as a result of "sewer service" (summonses not served in accordance with the law). Moreover, it was found that because of the inability of many people to understand the summons, especially among the Spanish-speaking population—some thinking that the summons was just another demand for payment—the summonses were ignored and default judgments were given to the creditors. As a result, New York State passed a law allowing the administrative judge to vacate default judgments against consumers who did not go to court because of sewer service, fear of the courts, or lack of counsel. In addition, the New York law was changed to compel the creditor in certain retail transactions to serve a summons written in both English and Spanish upon the judgment debtor.

If the debtor appears individually or through an attorney the summons and the defendant's answer are put in a file and the matter is "noticed for trial," that is, put down to await its day in court.

In court, there are various rules that must be adhered to by both the creditor and the debtor when presenting their cases. These rules are called "Rules of Evidence." Consequently, once the creditor goes into court he must be prepared to prove the indebtedness in order to secure a judgment against the debtor. For example, if he has sold merchandise to a debtor, the creditor must be prepared to show that he has a written contract, or that

5

he had made an oral offer and that acceptance was given by the debtor (even orally) to contract for or purchase the goods. Naturally, the simplest way to prove a contract is to show a written order with a description of the merchandise and all the terms of the sale. Next, the creditor must prove that he delivered the goods or the service to the debtor. That fact is most easily proved by a signed receipt.

In the absence of a valid written contract and a signed receipt of delivery, these facts must be established by witnesses or other legal proof. *It must be noted that the creditor or the party suing has the burden of proving his case; that is, he must tip the scales in favor of the facts he is attempting to prove.*

Before a judgment is obtained, the person seeking relief is called the plaintiff. If the judgment or decision is in his favor he is then called the judgment creditor. The person against whom the judgment was sought, the defendant, is then called the judgment debtor.

If the creditor obtains a judgment, a copy of the judgment is sent to the judgment debtor. If the debtor still refuses to pay, the judgment creditor's next step is to give an execution * (a written direction to satisfy the judgment out of the debtor's property) to the Sheriff (who is the state officer) or to the Marshal (who is usually a city officer). See Form #2 for form of execution. By law, however, certain property is exempt from execution. Our next chapter details all property that is exempt from or "untouchable" by an execution.

Unless specific property is mentioned in the execution, the Marshal or Sheriff will not look for any property of the judgment debtor and will return the execution to the court as "unsatisfied." This means that he has given up and cannot collect this judgment.

The law in most states, however, provides for various auxiliary methods of judgment collection. For example, the creditor can, through his attorney, examine the judgment debtor as to his assets. The examination is an informal hearing brought on by

---

* The States of Georgia, Delaware, Kentucky, Maryland, New Hampshire (writ of scire facias), Virginia, and West Virginia (writ of fieir facias) still use common law writs in enforcing judgments. All other states use a straight form of execution—but the results of either method are the same.

a subpoena to examine the judgment debtor. Ninety-nine percent of the time, however, the judgment debtor does not appear in answer to this subpoena, and if he does appear, he usually does not give all the facts to his creditor or to his creditor's attorney. The last chapter in this book describes other remedies that the judgment creditors can take for the enforcement of their judgments.

two

The Debtor's Rights and
Remedies Before He Is Sued and
Immediately After Suit
Is Brought Against Him

The debtor's immediate mental relief can be obtained if he will bear this one thought in mind.

You can never be put in jail for merely being in ordinary debt.

I say *ordinary* because the exceptions to this rule are being delinquent in the payment of alimony or in support payments for members of the family. However, even then, the debtor has to be found guilty of contempt of court before he can be jailed in a civil (not a criminal) jail. In other words, there has to be some showing that the debtor was contemptuous of the court and did not make payments although ordered to pay and able to pay. Therefore, if ever a creditor threatens you, Mr. Debtor, claiming that he can put you in prison or that he will put you in prison, he, the creditor, may be the one to go to jail—for "extortion." (See Chapter Nine.) Only the state can prosecute you for a crime, and being in debt is not a crime in any state.

Consequently, when you receive threatening telephone calls or letters, do not panic.

But, do not ignore your creditors.

If the creditor is malicious, slanderous, or commits an assault or battery on you, you may have a remedy as set forth in Chapter Nine of this book.

Moreover, many banking institutions and government agencies may not want to risk bad publicity by bringing suit against you. They will write one or two letters to you or try to contact you, and if that doesn't succeed, suit may never be instituted against you, *unless* you antagonize them by being unreasonable or outright nasty.

But if your creditor advises you that he is going to bring suit against you for your past-due debt, your best approach is to contact your creditor immediately. The purpose of contacting him immediately is to find out the basis of his action. "Play dumb" and let your creditor tell you what it's all about.

If you feel that his claim is unjust, or if you feel after reading this chapter that you have a defense that comes within one of the "affirmative defenses" listed below, your next move should be to inform the creditor of your knowledge of your legal rights and your defense. There is no question that once a creditor is aware that you know your legal rights and know what you are talking about, he will be less apt to strongly assert his rights. Then you are in a good position to settle the case, compromise the claim with him, or make your creditor simply forget about any claim against you.

DEFENSES

Debtor's rights include many legal defenses that justify not paying a debt. These defenses are legally referred to as "affirmative defenses." *However,* when a debtor is served with a summons, his affirmative defense must be set forth in answer to the summons and complaint served. Otherwise, the debtor will not be allowed to plead any of his affirmative defenses when he gets to court.

Affirmative defenses comprise many areas of law, and it is not within the limitations of this book to delve into each affirmative defense so as to cover the field of law completely. However, some of these defenses to a debt are as follows:

Usury

Usury can be defined as the charging of excess interest (more than the legal rate of interest) by a private person for the lending of money. In biblical days, to charge any interest was usury and was not allowed. As time went by, this strict rule was changed so that any rate of interest agreed upon by the borrower and lender was enforceable. Later, in order to protect needy borrowers from unscrupulous lenders, various usury laws were passed in England and thereafter in the United States. Each state, however, has its own legal rates of interest, which, when exceeded, will be usurious. For example, in New York State, the legal rate of simple interest is 8% a year. Consequently, if a contract is made in writing and shows on its face that more than 8% interest is to be paid, the agreement itself is usurious and, therefore, invalid or void. This means that the law declares that the lender should be barred from recovering any interest at all, but also lose his principal as well.

However, in some states the lender may avoid forfeiture of the principal sum by returning to the borrower the interest paid in excess of the lawful rate. In other states, excess of legal interest may be punishable as a crime; such states include California, Connecticut, Florida, Hawaii, Illinois, Kentucky, New

Mexico, New Jersey, New York, North Dakota, Rhode Island, South Carolina, South Dakota, Utah, Vermont, and Wisconsin. In New York, it is a crime to charge interest in excess of 25% per year.

The "contract rate" of interest is the rate agreed to by the parties for their contract. In many states, the parties may agree on a rate of interest that is higher than the "legal" rate. Usually such an agreement must be in writing and be signed by the borrower. But any agreed-to higher rate is also limited by law. For example, in Alabama, the legal rate of interest is 6% and the contract rate is limited to 8%. In Indiana, Maryland, New York, Pennsylvania, and West Virginia, the legal rate of interest is the same as the contract rate.

Maine, on the other hand, has no statutory provision nor any penalty concerning interest.

State legal rates of interest do *not* apply to banks, investment, or trust companies organized under the state law. Nor does the legal rate of interest apply to a borrowing corporation.

The laws affecting usury apply only to the interest paid *before* a loan matures. Therefore, any interest paid after final payment is due may not be usurious. For example, payments of more than the legal rate of interest as a penalty after the debt is past due are not usurious, nor is a loan agreement providing that the borrower pay attorneys' fees arising out of collection of the debt. The attorneys' fees, however, must be "reasonable," and if there is a dispute between the debtor and the creditor as to the reasonableness of the fees, a court may have to decide the issue.

Infancy

Generally, anyone under 21 years of age is considered legally an infant. However, various states have changed their laws to specify other ages. In Hawaii, for example, anyone under 20 years of age is an infant. In Kentucky, 18 years of age or under is considered infancy. In Alaska, a person under 19 years of age is considered an infant. In other states, a male under the age of 21 years is considered an infant while a female of 18, 19, or 20 may be considered an adult. In most states, however, a married female over the age of 18 is no longer considered an infant.

13

An "infant" may "assert his infancy" and therefore declare void any contract that is not for necessities. By necessities, we do not mean the food, shelter, and clothing that one needs just to survive. "Necessities" refers to the goods and services ordinarily needed to maintain one's social position or situation in life. Thus it is a relative term, and those items the law would consider necessities for one person might not be considered necessities for another person. However, a mere luxury can never be considered a necessity.

Although an infant may be entitled to any money that he has paid on a contract he declares void, he must return the goods received. For example, let us say that an 18-year-old buys a car under a conditional sales contract; he makes one payment and does not make any more. The finance company then sues on the promissory note. The infant can and should advise the dealer by certified mail that he is disaffirming or giving up the contract, and then return the car to the dealer.

Incompetency

A person who is legally adjudged mentally incompetent is not responsible for his debts, nor is a person who is so drunk at the time he incurs the debt that he does not know the nature of what he is doing.

But where the incompetent, insane, or drunkard has received the benefits of any agreement, his disability will be no defense to his debt. For example:

John Dry while drunk borrows $1,000 from Charlie Goodguy and gives Charlie a promissory note. The note calls for payment of the debt, plus 6% interest, in 60 days. When sued by Charlie for return of the $1,000 plus interest, John does not have as a legal defense the fact that he was drunk, because he has already received the benefits of the loan, that is, the money. Nor is there any evidence that Charlie took excessive interest or acted in such a way that one could say that he took advantage of John's being drunk.

Illegality

Any contract that is illegal or that is against the public policy of the state cannot be enforced. Most common in this category

14

are gambling debts. It is true that in some states such as Nevada, it may be the public policy of the state to enforce such debts, but in most states, debts incurred as a result of gambling are against public policy and, therefore, are unenforceable.

Public policy is usually reflected by the laws or statutes of a community. For example, for the protection of their citizens, most state laws require that certain professionals or business-men be licensed; these include doctors, attorneys, pawnbrokers, plumbers, barbers, real estate brokers, and many others. Conse-quently, a pawnbroker who has no license cannot withhold the property of his customers; an unlicensed real estate broker can-not collect a commission as a result of the sale of your home or any other real property.

Often, the question of what is "public policy" is difficult to answer. It depends upon the facts and circumstances of the times. In 1909, an action was brought by a seller for his purchase price of 42 volumes of the works of the French philosopher Voltaire. The defendant buyer claimed that he did not have to pay for the books because they contained "Licentious and Lurid material and could not be used by the defendant's family." The defendant claimed that the law then existing made it a crime to sell a publication that was immoral or obscene, and therefore the sale of any books containing that type of material was illegal. The trial court held that the works of Voltaire were immoral and that therefore the sales agreement was unenforceable. There is no question that today even the most moral of judges would not have found the works of Voltaire to be obscene and the sales contract would have been enforced against the buyer.

Statute of Limitations

In the early days of our common law, one having a claim against another could call the debtor into court at any time it suited his convenience. However, it was soon found that this practice caused great inconvenience and great injustice. The creditor or claimant may have waited until defense witnesses were dead or out of the jurisdiction of the court, or until papers were lost, or until the debtor himself died so that the claim might be enforced against his heirs.

To prevent these injustices, statutes of limitations were

15

enacted. With a statute of limitations, the creditor's right of action is limited to a specific length of time. Once again, each state varies not only with regard to the limitations of time in which to bring any civil action, but also with regard to the time within which to bring each of various types of actions. For example, in Alaska, the creditor has six years within which to bring an action on a promissory note after the note has fallen due. If an Alaskan wishes to bring an action on a contract, he has ten years in which to do so. In Illinois, a creditor has ten years in which to bring a suit on a promissory note and ten years in which to bring a suit on a contract; in Maryland, actions on promissory notes must be commenced within three years, but an action under a contract in Maryland may be commenced at any time up to twelve years from the date payment fell due.

Fraud

If you can show the court that the party instituting suit against you deceived you, and that because you relied on his promises or misrepresentation you were deprived of property or money, you may have a valid defense to the creditor's suit against you. However, one word of warning: The false promise or misrepresentation must be material—that is, significant rather than minor or the kind of sales puffery that is the stock in trade of nearly all sellers. Therefore, if a seller told you that the car he was selling you was "the best buy you can make," he was merely "sales-puffing," not making a material representation.

If, however, you were truly defrauded, you may not only have a valid defense to the action brought against you but also be able to *counterclaim* for treble damages. In some states treble damages are awarded as punishment to the party committing an unconscionable wrong.

Statute of Frauds

By specific statute and law, various kinds of contracts must be in writing in order to be enforced by a court. If one of the specified types of contracts is not in writing, it is voidable, and you may use the "statute of frauds" as an affirmative defense.

Remember, however, that the mere fact that a contract is not in writing does not mean that it is unenforceable. For example, if you hire someone to work for you for less than a year without having that

16

contract in writing, the employee can sue you to have the contract enforced.

Most state laws require that there be some sort of evidence in writing—a formal agreement or contract, letters or telegrams, or some note or memorandum—signed by the party against whom an action is brought in order for the following kinds of agreements to be enforceable by the courts:

(a) Any sale of land or real property must be in writing. This is required in all states of the United States, except Maryland, New Jersey, Pennsylvania, North Carolina, New Mexico, and Indiana.

In Maine, all leases concerning land or other real property must also be in writing. In all other states except Louisiana, leases for *over three years* must be in writing; in Louisiana oral leases are valid.

(b) Contracts for the sale of goods requiring payments of $500 or more are required to be in writing in every state. However, an exception is made where goods are to be made especially for the buyer if those goods cannot be sold in the ordinary course of the seller's business and the seller has made a substantial start in manufacturing (or procuring materials for the manufacture of) the goods. A contract for the purchase of such goods need not be in writing in order to be enforced by the seller against the buyer.

(c) A promise by an executor or an administrator of a decedent's estate must be in writing.

(d) In almost every state, an agreement not to be *completed* within one year, or an agreement that cannot be performed within one year, must be in writing in order to be enforced. However, in Mississippi, the requirement is extended to 15 months; North Carolina and Louisiana have no statute affecting this type of an agreement.

(e) The promise to pay a debt or to pay a default on a debt for another party must be in writing in every state. Delaware, however, requires that this type of guarantee or debt agreement need be in writing only if the debt is over $25.

Registered Trade Names and Corporations

Suppose you are sued by "Delicious Foods," a market with whom you have been dealing for quite some time. Disregarding the moral factor of whether or not you should pay for food you purchased, the fact that "Delicious Foods" is an unincorporated business owned by Harry Lamb, who is doing business under this trade name, will prevent Harry Lamb from suing and legally collecting against you if he has not filed a Certificate of Doing Business with the Clerk of the county in which his market is located. A check at the County Clerk's office will soon reveal whether or not he has formally so filed.

Moreover, if you are sued by an out-of-state corporation, you may have a defense if the corporation did not properly register its doing business certificate in your state. You may also have a defense even if the corporation is registered but does not have the legal power through its certificate of incorporation or charter to do the act or sell the product for which it seeks its claim against you.

Mistake or Duress

Contracts signed with the thought that you are buying one item when you are in reality buying another, may also be avoided by claiming mistake or no "mutuality of agreement."

By lack of mutuality of agreement, we mean that a contract is rendered void, as if it never came into being, where a mistake was made and as a result there was not a "meeting of the minds" of the parties to the agreement. Thus, owner calls his insurance broker to insure his horse, Speedy. But there are two horses called "Speedy" registered with the Thoroughbred Association, and the insurance company insures the wrong horse. No contract can result because there was no mutuality of agreement or meeting of the minds.

Even if the parties to a contract intend the same result but have each formed an untrue conclusion about an important part of the agreement, there is no true meeting of the minds or mutuality of agreement. Such a contract is void. For example, A and B both believe that a carton contains potatoes and they make a deal for its sale by A to B. Later, they discover that the carton contained tomatoes. The contract is voided because both parties were mistaken about an important element of the agreement.

Contracts signed under duress may be avoided by raising the affirmative defense of duress. In some states specific types of

18

contracts are outlawed by statute because such contracts are, by law, assumed to have been made by the buyer under duress or without his being able to fully understand their terms. For example, in California the "racket" of selling lifetime contracts for health studio services has been outlawed to the extent that no such contract shall be enforceable for more than $500. In New York, the Motor Vehicles Retail Installment Sales Act and the Retail Installment Sales Act regulate the retail installment sales of cars and of goods and services purchased on installment in New York. These laws specifically set forth the exact terms and obligations of these types of contract. Therefore, when confronted by a creditor who sold you a car or other retail purchase on an installment plan, you should ask him for a copy of the contract you signed and discuss this contract with your attorney. Your attorney may discover that the contract was not made in accordance with the law or that it was not signed by you in accordance with the laws designed for your protection.

Lack of Consideration

The mere oral promise by you to pay money to someone else is not sufficient reason for you to be legally responsible to pay that debt.

In most situations, a contract must be supported by "consideration." That is, there must be something in return for something. Consideration may be either something given or done, or something promised to be given or done in return for the other party's performance or promise. For example, you might simply promise to give your son-in-law $1,000. Your promise is unenforceable because you received no "consideration" from your son-in-law. Your promise to give $500 to some charity next year will likewise be unenforceable by a court because of the lack of consideration on the part of the charity. That is, neither your son-in-law nor the charity has given any consideration in return for your promise to pay.

Armed with the foregoing information about your "affirmative defenses," you should discuss with the creditor his claims against you. It may be that you will be able to convince the creditor that because of the good defenses you have he would be wasting his time in suing you. However, if your creditor is

19

not disturbed and insists upon his own rights, it may be that he has consulted his lawyer and knows of a defense to your defense. Then you had better run, not walk, to your attorney *immediately.*

Obligations of Other Members of the Family

Suppose your son has a fist fight in school and knocks out another boy's tooth. Are you responsible for your son's act? Must you pay the other boy's dental bills?

Suppose your wife goes to a local department store and orders a mink coat, when you can't even afford to buy her a cloth one. Are you personally responsible?

What if your young son, while playing in a Little League game, lets go of his bat and seriously injures a spectator. What would be your responsibility?

IN ALL THE PRECEDING SITUATIONS, YOU DO NOT HAVE A LEGAL *RESPONSIBILITY TO MAKE PAYMENT.*

Soldiers' and Sailors' Relief Act

If you are in the armed forces of the United States, or the public health service, or if you are a member of the immediate family of someone who is in one of those categories; or if you are a surety or guarantor or have endorsed a promissory note of someone in one of the above-mentioned categories, you may be protected by the Soldiers' and Sailors' Relief Act.

In 1940, Congress passed the Soldiers' and Sailors' Relief Act and amended it by the Selective Service Act of 1948. Through this legislation, relief is given to people in the aforementioned categories for the purpose of preventing any unjust seizure of their assets during their time of service.

The Soldiers' and Sailors' Relief Act, however, applies only to merchandise purchased before the customer joined the service. The purpose of the act is to be fair with those whose public duty does not give them the opportunity to defend a legal action against them. In order to protect servicemen, the statute affords (1) protection against default judgments, (2) a stay of proceedings—that is, the stopping of all suits or other proceedings at any stage, and (3) a stay of all foreclosures of chattels and mortgages.

The act provides protection against default judgments by

20

making it necessary for the judgment creditor to file an affidavit (sworn statement) that the debtor is not in military service. Making a false affidavit to obtain a default judgment is punishable by a $1,000 fine, or one year in prison, or both.

In addition, the Soldiers' and Sailors' Relief Act provides that at any stage of proceedings in court or in front of a municipal body, such proceedings may be stayed during the time the individual is in military service and for an additional sixty (60) days thereafter. In this regard, the courts are given power to stay any execution or garnishee or attachment.

Moreover, no person in military service can be evicted, nor can his property be taken for nonpayment of rent if the serviceman's rental is under $80 and the premises involved are used for living purposes for himself and/or his immediate family.

Proof of military service may be obtained in the following ways:

> For service in the Army, write the Adjutant General of the United States Army, Washington, D.C.
>
> For service in the Navy, write the Chief of Naval Personnel, Miscellaneous Service Branch, Enlisted Service & Records Division, Washington, D.C.
>
> For service in the Marines, write the Commandant of U.S. Marine Corps, Records Service Section Headquarters, Dep't. of Navy, Washington, D.C.
>
> For service in Air Force, write Air Adjutant General, Washington, D.C.
>
> For service in Coast Guard, write United States Coast Guard, Chief Administration Section, Commandant Headquarters, Washington, D.C.

three

Help From Consumer Protection Laws and Government Agencies

UNCONSCIONABLE CONTRACTS

The Uniform Commercial Code sets forth specifically the various rights and remedies of creditors, sellers, and purchasers. As of this writing all states except Louisiana have adopted the Code, sometimes slightly modifying some sections of it.

One of the least clearly interpreted sections of the Uniform Commercial Code deals with unconscionable contracts. The Code says: "If the Court, as a matter of law, finds the contract or any clause of the contract to have been unconscionable at the time it was made, the Court may refuse to enforce the contract, or it may enforce the remainder of the contract without the unconscionable clause, or it may so limit the application of any unconscionable clause as to avoid any unconscionable result." Therefore, this section of the law permits the courts in states that have adopted the Code to police unfair contracts.

Some of the questions the courts have considered are the following:

1. Were important terms of the contract hidden in a maze of fine print or through deceptive practices made to seem unimportant?
2. Did each party to the contract understand the terms of the contract?
3. Was the price charged by the seller exorbitant—perhaps two, three, or even five times the amount of the usual purchase price?
4. Was the representation of the value far in excess of the actual value?

The question of whether or not a contract is unfair does not go to a jury. Instead it is determined by the judge. (It should be noted that the party who loses can bring his case to an appellate court for review.) This section of the Code does not provide for damages. The most the injured party can achieve under this section is a direction by the Court that the contract, or a part of the contract, cannot be enforced against him.

Les us look at some recent cases concerning the law of "unconscionable" contracts. The courts in some states, for example, have held that a home improvement contract is unconscionable if at the time of the sale the seller fails to furnish a clear and concise statement setting forth the finance charges that the home owner will have to pay for goods and services—especially where the costs were in excess of $2,500 and goods and services were worth substantially less.

In another type of case a Spanish-speaking buyer was told by a Spanish-speaking salesman that an appliance which the buyer claimed he could not afford to buy would cost him and his wife nothing, because each of them would be paid a $25 commission on every sale made to their neighbors and friends. However, the contract submitted to and signed by the buyer was in English, but it was neither translated nor explained to him. The buyer later realized that the contract actually provided for a cash sales price of $1,500, to which there was added a credit service charge of $350. In court it was shown that the seller knew the retail value of the appliance was $450. The Court decreed that the contract constituted too harsh a bargain and it would not be enforced as written.

Whenever there is language barrier, as, for example, when a buyer has a very limited command of the English language, a contract in English that he signs *may* be declared unconscionable if it is unfair or if it is shown that its terms are substantially different from what the buyer thought them to be. However, courts often hold that the buyer who does not understand English well has a duty to have the contract translated for him into his native language before he signs it. Yet if the buyer can show that the seller unfairly induced him to sign the contract without having it translated, or if the seller had it translated incorrectly for the buyer, the buyer has a better chance to have the Court declare the contract to be unconscionable.

Another type of case involved an appliance, which an expert witness testified had a maximum value of $300 but which was sold for over $1,000. This exorbitant price made the contract unconscionable, and therefore, unenforceable. The courts have consistently held that an excessively high price may constitute an unconscionable contract within the meaning of the Uniform Commercial Code. Retail installment contracts charging the buyer from two to six times the cost of the goods to the seller are particularly vulnerable to being declared unconscionable and therefore unenforceable.

One buyer paid $950 plus a credit service charge of $240 for a 1968 Plymouth, and then had to spend $700 to repair defects that had existed at the time of the purchase. The Court declared that he was entitled to a reasonable opportunity as provided by the Uniform Commercial Code to present evidence to aid the Court in determining the issue of unconscionability.

Where a contract for rental of a truck made the lessee absolutely liable for all damages to the truck, regardless of his own fault, such a contract was unconscionable.

Any contract signed by the buyer in which the seller *waived* his liability to sell the buyer a car warranted for "fitness of purpose," that is, good enough to be driven for a reasonable period of time given the age and obvious condition of the car, would be unconscionable and unenforceable between the buyer and the seller.

The courts have also held that it is unconscionable for a contract to permit the seller to retain possession of repossessed goods and collect a repossession fee after the buyer had made good an installment past due.

However, it is to be noted that the fact that one party makes a large profit and the other party runs risks does not of itself make the contract unconscionable. If the parties had equal bargaining power—especially if the buyer could have gotten a better deal elsewhere if he didn't like the terms presented to him—and if the contract was freely entered into after reasonable negotiation, the Court probably will not declare it unconscionable.

Still another type of case involved the purchase of "food plans." Because of the wording of the installment contract (usually in small print), the buyer believed he was buying only a food plan. The food sold was usually less expensive than the same food bought in the supermarket, and the salesman represented that a freezer was "given free" or, in effect, that it was free because of the monetary savings from the food plan. In reality, however, the purchaser was actually buying a freezer for perhaps six or seven times its value (for example, a $200 freezer for $1,200), and *also* signing a contract to buy food under the food plan. After the contract was made, the seller usually sold it to a finance company or bank. Thus that institution then had the claim against the purchaser, whom we should now call "debtor." The purchaser of the contract (a finance company or bank) then notified the purchaser that it had taken over the contract.

However, it is the law in most states that if the debtor on a retail installment contract has a claim against a seller of goods or services who has sold a contract to a third party, the debtor must give notice of his claim to the purchaser of the contract within ten days of the date on which the purchaser of the contract mailed its notice telling the debtor that it had taken over the contract. Therefore, if the debtor has a good claim against the seller of the goods or services but does nothing about notifying the bank or finance company within ten days after the institution mails a notice to him that it is now collecting against the contract, the debtor has no remedy against either the seller or the institution that bought the contract.

Under the law of unconscionable contracts, however, you may avoid payment of the debt if you can show that the seller *knew* his contract was unconscionable (as described above), or if the institution that bought the contract was so intimately involved with the seller that they were, in effect, one and the same company so that the finance institution can be said to have taken part in the fraud perpetrated by the seller against the debtor.

> NOTE: The unconscionable contract defense must be properly pleaded in order to be successful, and it is well to consult a lawyer if you believe you have a case to which it applies.

THE FEDERAL TRUTH IN LENDING LAW

The Federal Truth in Lending Law is the popular name for Public Law 90–321. It was designed to conform each state's regulation of consumer credit to the policies of the Federal government and in this case to the Federal act and its regulations. The essential purpose of the Truth in Lending Law is to protect the consumer from exorbitant finance charges by letting the consumer know what the charge is so he can compare finance charges of various companies. *The Truth in Lending Law does not fix interest rates on credit charges. Your state may have a law setting such limits.*

Regulation "Z" of the law applies to banks, savings and loan associations, department stores, credit card issuers, credit unions, automobile dealers, consumer finance companies, residential mortgage brokers, and residential craftsmen (such as plumbers and electricians). It also applies to physicians, dentists, and other professional people, to hospitals, and to any other organization or individual who extends or arranges credit which is payable in more than *four* installments for which a finance charge is or may be payable.

Under the law, the rate of simple interest may be stated in percentages on any finance agreement—e.g., interest is being charged at the rate of 6%, 5%, and so on. In addition, the dollar and cents total finance charge must be typed or written into the agreement as must the annual percentage of compound interest charged. The words "annual percentage rate" must stand out especially clear.

The law does *not* apply to credit extended for business or commercial purposes, except agricultural credit. It does not apply to credit extended to Federal, state, and other governmental agencies. Nor does it apply to transactions with a broker in securities or commodities.

Generally, the Truth in Lending Law (under Regulation Z) applies to credit not exceeding $25,000 extended to people for family, personal, household, or agricultural use. However, *all* real estate credit transactions—regardless of the amount—are also covered.

A party who is damaged under a contract to which the Federal Truth in Lending Law applies may sue for twice the amount of the finance charge, or a minimum of $100, to a maximum of $1,000, in addition to court costs and his attorney's fee. This means that if, for example, a businessman sells a product and does not comply with the Truth in Lending Law, because he has not disclosed his finance charges as required by the law, or if he has falsely advertised contrary to the law, the consumer defrauded of, say, $6 can sue and, if he wins, collect a minimum of $100, plus attorney's fees and court costs. The violator who willfully and knowingly disobeys the law or any of its regulations can also be fined up to $5,000 or imprisoned for one year or both.

Various agencies of the United States government have been

set up to deal with the Truth in Lending Law. Contact these agencies; they will help you if you have a problem or question, or wish to bring a complaint under this act. The following agencies are responsible for enforcing Regulation "Z."

With any problem concerning:

National banks, consult the Controller of Currency, United States Treasury Department, Washington, D.C. 20220.

State member banks, see the Federal Reserve Bank serving the area in the state where bank is located.

Nonmember insured banks, contact the Federal Deposit Insurance Corporation's Supervising Examiner for the district in which the nonmember insured bank is located.

Federal credit unions, contact the regional office of the Bureau of Federal Credit Unions serving the area in which the Federal credit union is located.

Creditors subject to the Civil Aeronautics Board, contact the Director of the Bureau of Enforcement, Civil Aeronautics Board, 1825 Connecticut Avenue, N.W., Washington, D.C. 20428.

Creditors subject to the Interstate Commerce Commission, contact the Office of Proceedings, Interstate Commerce Commission, Washington, D.C. 20523.

Retail department stores, consumer finance companies, and all other creditors which are controlled by Truth in Lending, contact the Division of Consumer Credit, Federal Trade Commission, Washington, D.C. 20580.

You will note that the remedy given to the consumer for being the victim of a violation of the Truth in Lending Law makes it mandatory that the injured party, himself, must sue. The Federal agencies listed above can give you information about your rights but they cannot sue your creditor for you. *If you are successful* in your own suit, however, you can recover your attorney's fees and court costs in addition to money damages.

OTHER FEDERAL CONSUMER PROTECTION LAWS

There are also other Federal statutes for the protection of the consumer. For example, the Radiation Control Act sets standards for radiation emission from various products. If television sets produce X-rays or radiation in excess of the amount allowed, retailers are directed to recall all such sets sold by them. The Tire Recall Bill also provides for a quick recall system for tires found to be dangerous or defective. The Flammable Products Act regulates all wearing apparel, as well as fabrics used in the home, including rugs, drapes, and linens; the Department of Commerce has regulations for manufacturers' testing of the flammability of these products. The Child Protection Act gives power to the Department of Health, Education and Welfare to regulate all electrical, mechanical, and thermal articles used by children. But in none of these acts is the Federal government given the power to bring any civil suit on behalf of the injured citizen.

However, it is to be noted that if a person is injured as a result of a violation of any of the provisions of the foregoing laws, he may take advantage of the appropriate law in his own suit in negligence. For example, little Mary Jones is given a new dress for her seventh birthday. However, the dress was made of a highly flammable fiber, contrary to the Flammable Products Act. When Mary lights the candles on her birthday cake, she accidentally drops the lighted candle she is holding and her dress catches fire, causing severe burns. Mere violation of the statute can mean that the manufacturer of the inflammable dress and the store from which the dress was purchased are liable for negligence and/or breach of warranty. Negligence may not even have to be proved, because proof of violation of the statute can make out a good case against the manufacturer and anyone handling this unlawful product.

Other Federal statutes, such as the Food, Drug and Cosmetic Act, provide that violators of the act are given stringent penalties and may be criminally prosecuted. So if you have been hurt by any violation of the Food, Drug and Cosmetic Act, you may have a civil action against the perpetrator—that is, an action for money damages—even though he had no knowledge that he was violating the act, and the violator may even face jail as a result of a criminal case against him by the Federal government.

STATE AND LOCAL LAWS AND REGULATIONS

The trend today in statutes intended to protect the consumer is to fine any violator. New York State, for example, recently passed a statute giving the state power to seek $500 from each false advertiser or other party guilty of any deceptive practice under the Deceptive Practice Act. However, false advertising and fraudulent sales practices are difficult to prosecute criminally, and today most district attorneys are much too busy with more serious crimes to bother with deceptive practices and false advertising. As a result, many state and local governments have set up consumer fraud bureaus.

Most localities give their consumer fraud bureau agencies many remedies to protect and help the defrauded consumer. For example, consumer fraud bureaus have the power to seek temporary injunctions; that is, they can go into court for an order to restrain a nefarious company from its deceptive practices.

In addition, many cities and states have passed consumer protection laws that allow the agencies assigned to enforce the laws to sue offenders on behalf of the injured party and to obtain refunds for deceived customers.

Local government agencies or departments also license many businesses that deal with consumers. Through this licensing power, they can control a fraudulent or "unconscionable" practice on the part of a seller whose business they have licensed. As a result of a complaint made by a defrauded party, and after an investigation is made by the appropriate agency, the overreaching businessman, rather than lose his license, would undoubtedly promise not only to stop further "fraudulent" or overreaching practices, but also to make restitution of any money lost by the complainant.

A fine example of a consumer protection law is that passed by the City Council of New York City in December, 1969. This law prohibits all forms of false advertising and false statements in the sale of goods and services, as well as practices which the Commission of Consumer Affairs defines as "unconscionable." With the blessing of the courts, the New York City Department of Consumer Affairs has the unique authority to issue regulations prohibiting grossly unfair business conduct, as well as to prevent deceptive practices. The City Council provided that a violation of the law can be punished by a fine of $1,000.

Regulation 4 of New York City's Consumer Protection Law also prohibits creditors from communicating with debtor's employers. The practice of sending letters to the employers of alleged debtors is a substantial violation of a consumer's personal privacy as well as a threat to his job. Unfortunately, however, most employees do not know their rights, and the practice of intimidating employees through their employer continues. If such intimidation happens to you, contact the Department of Consumer Affairs.

The New York City Department of Consumer Affairs also has regulations to prohibit false statements in collection letters and unfounded threats to drive debtors to pay claims which may be unjust. According to former Department of Consumer Affairs Commissioner, Bess Myerson, one furniture company sent a buyer a telegram saying that unless she paid her debt immediately, "the City Marshal would break down the door and take everything." That statement was patently false, because a city marshal, or anyone else, in fact, cannot enter anyone's home without the resident's permission. Furthermore, a city marshall cannot act without a judgment being entered and an execution issued against property.

The New York City Department of Consumer Affairs has received a great many complaints about concerns that have delayed delivery, have delivered defective merchandise, or have failed to make repairs as promised. One couple ordered some furniture that was delivered unfinished, many months later. For over a year, the couple tried to get different furniture. Finally, they contacted the Department of Consumer Affairs and obtained a full refund through them.

The Commissioner stated that contractors often take on much more work than they can handle—some accept as many as 40 jobs for one month with the knowledge that only 12 jobs can be completed. That means that consumers have to wait six months or longer for completion of work they were told would be done immediately. One company, for example, entered into a contract for $4,200 in April, promising completion of the job by June. In May, the couple had paid $1,400 to the contractor; by the end of June, no work had even started. This injured couple then turned to the Civil Court and sued the contractor. A judgment was secured, but because the firm had no assets, the complainants were unable to get their money. However, through the Department of Consumer Affairs' power to fine, the couple was successful. The department also revoked the contractor's license.

Another contractor had been selling burglar alarms on credit

33

in low-income neighborhoods and misrepresenting to consumers that the alarm would ring in the police station. When a consumer found out that this was not so, he usually stopped making his installment payments. As a result, the contractor would file a lawsuit. In fact, this particular contractor was said to have sued more people than any other seller of goods in New York City. When complaints were made to the Department of Consumer Affairs, the department contacted the contractor and reached a "consent judgment" with him to give refunds to those people who had made legitimate complaints. This "consent judgment" could be enforced by the city agency only because of its licensing power over contractors (the penalty for operating as a contractor without a license is imprisonment for up to six months and a maximum fine of $1,000).

In another case, a young man signed a contract for karate lessons. After having only one lesson, he found that karate was a bit too strenuous for his weak frame—despite representations that "it is nothing but child's play." The contract which this daring young man had signed but now wished to disaffirm was a contract for one year's lessons for over $800. Yes, he was told, he could drop out after a single lesson, but the whole contract price must be paid, less 20%.

As a result of such "service rackets" various agencies throughout the country have passed regulations limiting the charges for drop-outs. Prior to the adoption of these regulations, numerous complaints had been made by consumers under these service contracts because they had been told by the salesman that they could cancel "without penalty," when, as a matter of fact, there either was no cancellation provision in the contract or a heavy cancellation fee was assessed when the consumer left the school during the course of instruction. The new regulations usually provide that the seller of the "future service" contract must disclose the cancellation provision in the contract to the consumer within a certain number of days after a contract is cancelled. If the consumer complains to the appropriate agency, the seller must return to the buyer any payments made in excess of the amount permitted to be retained under the regulations. Here again, the consumer can be protected and can get out of debt without resort to a lawsuit but merely by a complaint to the proper agency.

34

One company enticed expectant mothers to "baby planning" parties. Complaints were received from many pregnant women throughout the city of New York whose hopes had been inflated by promises of a free crib if they attended such a "party." The only thing that the company delivered was a sales pitch for over-priced baby furniture.

This company obtained the names of expectant parents either by purchasing mailing lists or by promising other customers that $5 would be deducted from their bills for every name of a pregnant woman they supplied to the salesman (although that promise was made only if the customers balked at the prices and was never written into their contracts). The company then sent parents-to-be an invitation to a "baby planning" party, usually held at a major motel. The company's deception started with its first letter. The letterhead on the invitation showed a company name and an address at which, in fact, there was no such company doing business. The invitation was worded to convey the impression that the purpose of the party was to give expectant parents valuable information about how to care for their baby. One consumer wrote the department that she and her husband first believed that this was a government-sponsored prenatal program. The invitation mentioned a film on baby safety, a lecture on baby care by a nurse, and a question-and-answer period. There was no indication that any attempt would be made to sell baby furniture, but the invitations did promise a free "junior crib" to all couples who attended.

Approximately 30 couples attended each party. Each couple was seated at a table with a salesman, thus isolated from other guests at the party and subject to a maximum sales pitch. The salesmen did reproduce the *atmosphere* of the party, and a film on baby safety was shown. Then each salesman employed the pressure tactics on his couple, offering them a *fictitious* discount: the customers could pay for the baby furniture in four installments.

A lawsuit brought by the Consumer Fraud Bureau asked that this company be forced to halt its deceptive practices and the consumers who were cheated had their money returned.

Now regulations of this government agency make it an "unconscionable practice" for a person or business entity to set up or operate "an endless chain scheme." A chain or "pyramid" scheme is a get-rich-quick scheme that has cropped up all over the country and caused unwary consumers hundreds of thousands of dollars. This scheme is a device by which buyers of a product try to make money by finding fresh victims and selling them either the product itself or the right to sell it. Pyramid sales operations work on the same principle as chain letters: to produce a chain of buyers and sellers of a product, a service, or a franchise. Each buyer has the right to sell the product, service, or franchise to other buyers, and each of these sellers to still others. Eventually a vast pyramid of sellers is supposed to be formed, with those near the top striking it rich. The pyramid collapses when the supply of available participants within a certain limited area is exhausted. The Department of Consumer Affairs pointed out that in Manhattan, for example, if each of the hundred distributors sign up five people, and each of these sold to five more, every family in the borough would own a distributorship after five rounds of selling. Here again is an example of how people easily get into debt by being tricked into a scheme. However, a complaint to the proper authority will in all probability get the victim out of debt.

CLASS ACTION SUITS

Some statutes also give government agencies the power to seek *mass restitution.* By this power, the protective agency can institute an action in court on behalf of everyone who has a valid complaint of injury and set up a fund to distribute money received for all those who have complained.

Moreover, under comparatively new statutes, the individual consumer has the additional right of a "class" action for actual damages caused by a prohibited practice or a pattern of violation. That is, a single individual who has suffered damages can sue the violator of the law on behalf of himself and all other people similarly damaged by the violation, that is, on behalf of a "class" of people. If the plaintiff wins the case, the money damages awarded are put into a fund and are paid out to all members of the class who have proved their claim. In addition to this, the Federal Truth in Lending Law provides that attorneys' fees may be awarded if the consumer wins his case. The provision of attorneys' fees is a great stimulus to the consumer who may not have the money to hire an attorney to bring an action.

Rule 23 of the Federal Rules of Civil Procedure gives more liberal construction to the use of class actions than our state procedural laws; consequently, there is a greater incentive for attorneys to take only those cases that can be brought in the Federal courts. However, there are many bills in Congress and in the state legislatures at the present time to allow more liberal class actions in state courts and the payment of attorneys' fees upon success. The passage of such new laws will give the consumer greater opportunity for personal recovery.

A list of state and local consumer protection agencies is included as Exhibit 2 in the Appendix. Please note that the powers and responsibilities of these governmental agencies vary. If there is no listed agency in your county or immediate vicinity, contact the attorney general's office in your state. The attorney general will put you in touch with the specific agency that will help you. Don't be at all hesitant to contact these agencies. Their very purpose is to protect your rights.

four

Can the Debtor Do
Anything About . . .

THE HOLDER IN DUE COURSE DOCTRINE

For some time, Mrs. Agnes Jones had been thinking of renovating her kitchen. Her sink was old-fashioned and rusty; she needed more cabinets for her dishes and pots and pans; it was always so hot in the kitchen that a blower for ventilation was needed; and she wanted a garbage disposal unit. So, one day, when Charlie Sharpshooter knocked on her door offering her a new kitchen for $4,500, she was an easy selling mark—especially so, since she and her husband had long since priced these renovations at $6,500. That evening, therefore, she signed a contract with the salesman for $4,500. Much to her future sorrow, however, she did not know that Charlie Sharpshooter was an "independent" who subcontracted the job; that is, gave out the order to a contractor to handle and then sold the contract from Agnes Jones to "Federal Safety Bank." The bank then sent Mrs. Jones a promissory note for the amount of the contract and a payment book for the installment payments.

A few days after the kitchen was "installed," Mrs. Jones found that the disposal unit no longer functioned and the wood of her cabinets had begun to split.

Mrs. Jones tried to phone the contractor, but he was nowhere to be found. When the first installment was due to the bank, Mrs. Jones, on advice from her neighbor, Mr. Smith (whose sister worked for an attorney), did not make the payment. As a result, she received a notice from the bank that the installment was due, and that there were late charges as well. But Mrs. Jones made no payments whatsoever to the bank because she felt secure in the fact that the disposal unit did not work (and she had witnesses) and that the cabinets were broken (and she had witnesses). And so, three months went by. Then, lo and behold, one day she was served with a summons by the bank, not only for the amount due under the contract, but also for attorneys' fees, interest, and court costs under the note she had signed. Then Mrs. Jones went to a lawyer. Her attorney advised her that the bank is a "holder in due course," which means that the bank had taken the contract in good faith and without notice of any existing defense or claim on the part of Mrs. Jones.

Under the law in most states, it is the obligation of the bank (or a finance company) as the purchaser of an installment contract, to issue a notice by mail of the sale of the installment contract. This notice requires the buyer, in this case Mrs. Jones, to notify the bank of any existing claims or any defenses she may have (of bad workmanship, etc.) *within ten days of mailing of such notice.* Since Mrs. Jones had not so notified the bank, she had no claim or defense against the bank for any of the slipshod work or malfunctions in her kitchen.

Many states have legislation pending to extend this ten-day period to three or four months to give a defrauded party such as Mrs. Jones an opportunity to air her grievances and have them corrected. Today, unfortunately, most banks and finance companies are not too concerned about whom they purchase installment contracts from, because, even though the law requires that the installment sales contract specify that Mrs. Jones has ten days after notice from the bank or finance company to notify it of any grievance, in all likelihood Mrs. Jones either will not notice any defects or will pay no attention to defects within that short time. If the time were extended to three or four months, the banks and finance companies would be more careful about the people from whom they purchase such contracts.

One note of optimism is the fact that under the Federal Consumer Protection Act (Truth in Lending Law), a three-day "cooling off" period is provided on certain installment transactions. During that time the contract may be rescinded by the debtor. However, the present law only applies where a *security interest in realty* is given as collateral for a consumer credit transaction. Form 1 in the Appendix presents a copy of a notice to the consumer required by the Federal law in this type of transaction. You will note that the form provides that you as a customer can execute the right to rescind within three business days from the date of the contract and not be liable for any finance or other charges. Form 1 itself can be used if you wish to rescind within the three days' time.

Under Regulation "Z" (which is a document issued by the Federal Reserve Board telling the seller of merchandise on credit how to comply with the Truth in Lending Law), these forms of notice are suggested to the seller of merchandise, and

42

any form you receive from a seller on credit should conform to these forms or contain all the information set forth in them.

UNSOLICITED MERCHANDISE SENT THROUGH THE MAIL

Many charitable as well as commercial organizations send free merchandise through the mail. If you did not solicit this merchandise, you have no obligation to return it. Not only may you keep unsolicited merchandise sent to you through the mail, you do not owe the sender one cent for it. Under our law, you may regard this merchandise as a gift. In fact, in many states it is illegal for any concern to send unsolicited merchandise.

LOST, STOLEN, OR MISUSED CREDIT CARDS

The lawsuits involving credit cards are primarily the result of lost, stolen, or misused credit cards.

Many states have passed laws limiting the obligations of the owner of a credit card that is lost or stolen. These statutes usually provide that the credit card owner's liability is limited from the time he gives written notice to the issuer of the card. In addition, statutes in various states limit the liability of the owner of the credit card for its unauthorized use. In New York, for example, the limitation is $250. In North Dakota, Vermont, and Minnesota, the limit of liability for unauthorized use is $100; in Massachusetts, New Mexico, and New Jersey, similar laws limit the liability to $50; the Illinois limit is $25.

It may be stated as a general rule of thumb that the owner of a lost or stolen credit card is not liable for purchases made by a wrongful user if the owner immediately notifies the issuer of the credit card. However, whether or not the owner of a credit card knew that his card had been stolen or lost at the time it was used by someone else is a question of fact that has to be determined if suit is brought against the owner for payment. In one case, for example, an owner was unaware of the loss or theft of his card and so did not give notice as required by law. In that case, 237 purchases were made with the owner's card within a period of one month. However, there was no evidence that the owner failed to exercise reasonable care or that she had authorized anyone to act in her behalf. Consequently, the owner of the card was held not liable for the unauthorized purchases. If, however, it can be shown that the credit card owner was careless in the use and custody of his card or that he indiscriminately gave his card to others, he can be held responsible for the purchases made by the user.

Remember, the most important remedy available to a credit card holder when his card is lost or stolen is written notice to the issuer of the card. It is suggested that such notice be sent by certified or registered mail with a return receipt requested, so that the credit card owner has a receipt showing that the issuer received due notification of the lost or stolen card.

If a credit card owner gives another person permission to use his credit card, the owner will be responsible for the purchases made, even if the person to whom he gave his credit card exceeded his authority. For example, John gave his credit card to his girl friend, Mary, with permission to purchase anything up to $100. Mary purchased a ring for $200. The cases involving similar situations indicate John responsible for Mary's purchase of $200.

If you are a retail dealer it is incumbent upon you to ascertain whether or not a credit card has been reported lost or stolen. If you honor a card knowing that it is being wrongfully used, this knowledge would be a defense by the credit card issuer in an action by the retailer.

COMPLAINTS TO MANUFACTURERS

How many times have you heard a friend or neighbor complain that despite the fact that he has taken his new car back to his dealer at least half a dozen times, the car still leaks water, has a faulty starter or rattling windows or some other defect. Sure, he can sue for breach of the "warranty of fitness." But it costs money to bring suit and it may take quite some time before his case comes to court. Meanwhile the car may be so mechanically defective that he cannot use it. Or a man with a small business may have gone into debt to purchase a truck or some other equipment but because of defects it cannot be used immediately. As a result, his new business may be placed in jeopardy and he may be put much deeper into debt to other creditors.

The United States Office of Consumer Affairs claims that the number one complaint to most state and local consumer protective offices concerns automobiles. As a result, the Automotive Consumer Action Panels (Auto CAPS), an association of automobile dealers, attempts to provide a speedy and fair solution to problems not solved by the dealer or manufacturer. If you live within an area covered by these trade associations and have a problem that the manufacturer or dealer has not resolved to your satisfaction, you should contact your local association. When stating your problem, document your facts with receipts, bills, letters, cancelled checks, and/or pictures of your car.

Here are the addresses and telephone numbers of participating automobile dealer associations:

Automotive Trade Association, National Capital Area
Suite 505, 8401 Connecticut Avenue
Chevy Chase, Maryland 20015
Telephone: 301–652–6945

Cleveland Automobile Dealers Association
310 Lakeside Avenue, N.W.
Cleveland, Ohio 44114
Telephone: 216–241–2880

Metropolitan Denver Automobile Dealers Association
Suite 101, 70 W. 6th Avenue
Denver, Colorado 80204
Telephone: 303–534–8249

Oregon Automobile Dealers Association
Box 14460
Portland, Oregon 97214
Telephone: 503–233–5044

Orlando Automobile & Truck Dealers
Suite #221, 1350 Orange Avenue
Winter Park, Florida 32789
Telephone: 305–647–5100

Pennsylvania Automotive Association
Box 2955
Harrisburg, Pennsylvania 17105
Telephone: 717–232–1931

Utah Automobile Dealers Association
Box 1019
Salt Lake City, Utah 84101
Telephone: 801-355-7473

If you do not live in an area where there is an Auto CAPS group and if your dealer has not helped you, it is a good idea for those having legitimate complaints to contact the manufacturer directly. In fact, a letter directed to the personal attention of the president of the manufacturing corporation will be most effective. But one word of warning: Make your letter short, concise, and to the point; *and above all, set forth all the facts briefly, stated without emotion.* Remember, the president of any responsible manufacturing company should be interested in knowing what defects there are in his product.

If, after a reasonable time, you do not hear from the president or any employee to whom he may have assigned your letter (most companies try to answer complaint letters within three weeks), then—*and only then*—should you "raise the roof." You can create a rumpus by contacting your local radio station or newspaper, the appropriate local agency of your state attorney general's office, the state attorney general's office itself, or the other governmental agencies about which we speak in this book. Then, if you still get no satisfactory response from the manufacturer, get yourself an attorney and determine whether or not to bring a lawsuit.

GUARANTOR'S LIABILITY FOR BANK LOANS

Ed Goodfellow agreed to guarantee a loan of $3,100 for his son-in-law. The bank approved a loan for $1,200. Ed's son-in-law defaulted on the loan and the bank tried to get the money from Ed. The Court held, however, that Ed was not responsible as a guarantor on the loan. The Court stated that even though Ed had signed the promissory note, "it is apparent that the guarantor [Ed] did not agree to the sum thereafter inserted by the bank in a promissory note." Ed had agreed to guarantee a loan for $3,100, not for $1,200. Therefore, having not consented to the loan actually given, even though it was for a lesser

46

amount than he had agreed to, Ed was not a guarantor for the loan.

ENFORCEMENT OF JUDGMENTS ON CLAIMS BY CORPORATIONS OR COLLECTION AGENCIES

Certain people, among them various collection agencies, make a practice of purchasing judgments long outstanding and then executing against the homes and property of the affected judgment debtors. Since a collection agency's business is to collect money for creditors, it is engaging in an unauthorized practice of law when it seeks, on its own behalf, to execute against a debtor's property.

Statutes enacted in New York and many other states seek to forestall the unauthorized practice of law in order to lessen the promotion of lawsuits by attorneys and to discourage the use of legal process to harass and embarrass debtors. Under these laws, any attempt by a collection agency or an individual to enforce a *purchased* judgment by execution against a debtor's property can be frustrated. However, for the debtor to be successful, he has to prove two essential elements:

1. that the party seeking to execute against him and enforce the judgment is—directly or indirectly—in the business of collection and adjustment of claims, and
2. that the judgment was purchased "for the purpose of bringing an action or proceeding thereon." The courts interpret the word "proceeding" broadly enough to cover execution or any other legal action for the collection of a judgment.

If the court finds that these two essentials are present, the assignment of the judgment is void and, therefore, any execution resulting from the purchase of the judgment is likewise void.

STOCKBROKERS' "CHURNING"

Churning is the practice by which an unethical broker induces a customer over whose account he has some control, to

47

purchase stocks primarily for the purpose of increasing the broker's commissions. This practice is one of the four types of evils that Rule 405 of the New York Stock Exchange seeks to control.

Rule 405 states, in essence, that New York Stock Exchange brokers must "know their customers and the source of their funds." The purpose of this rule undoubtedly is to make brokerage firms responsible for:

1. investigating the source of the funds that their customers use in trading,
2. supervising their representatives and salesmen, and
3. honestly analyzing the suitability of the stocks they select for their customers.

Thus it may be that a salesman for a stock brokerage house recommends to a "friend" a very speculative bond issue that costs the customer the last $5,000 to his name; such a salesman might be guilty of churning. So too, a salesman may be guilty of churning if, having been given $15,000 by a busy doctor to "just make me some money," the salesman—even though he makes money for his customer—repeatedly buys and sells the same stock so many times that it is obvious he simply bought and sold to make his commissions on the deals.

Certainly a buyer of stocks cannot allow himself to be "duped" into buying a highly speculative stock and then, only if the stock goes down, seek protection under Rule 405. However, if the customer actually lost the amount of his investment because of "churning" he may seek damages for the amount lost, or, where churning was maliciously practiced, for the amount lost plus punitive damages.

BLOCKBUSTING

"Blockbusting" is the practice of certain real estate brokers and salesmen of getting the owners of residential property to sell their property to them or to their associates by creating an atmosphere of fear that their home values are depreciating due to the prospective or the present entry into the neighborhood of a different ethnic group, race, or religion.

For example, Joe Sharp, a real estate operator, called on Mrs.

48

Mary Wilson, who had recently been widowed. Sharp told Mrs. Wilson that because he had known and liked her husband, he had come to warn her that she should sell her house before it depreciated in value. A minority group family was moving into the next block and a similar family was coming to her own street, he told her. Mrs. Wilson became panicky, and she soon signed a contract to sell her $30,000 home to Sharp for $21,000. Since Mrs. Wilson's mortgage was for $17,000, after closing fees she was left with only $3,800. With her very small income and the high apartment rental she now had to carry, Mrs. Wilson was soon deeply in debt. You may feel that Mrs. Wilson should not have been reluctant to live in a "mixed" neighborhood. Nonetheless, Mrs. Wilson was only one of many victims of unscrupulous real estate agents who generate and then exploit fear and panic in a neighborhood.

In New York State, the Department of State is the governmental agency empowered with the licensing and disciplining of real estate brokers and salesmen. In an effort to stop blockbusting, the secretary of state of the state of New York issued a directive in 1971 forbidding licensed real estate brokers and salesmen from soliciting in certain sections of New York City. (The non-solicitation sections are East Flatbush and Crown Heights in Brooklyn and Cambria Heights and Laurelton in Queens.) If, therefore, realtor Joe Sharp had violated this directive, because Mary Wilson lived within the boundaries indicated in it, Mrs. Wilson's complaint to the Department of State would result in an order for immediate restitution to her of her loss.

LANDLORD/TENANT PROBLEMS

The state of New Jersey recently passed a "Tenant Reciprocal Law." California, Connecticut, Delaware, Hawaii, Illinois, Maine, Maryland, Massachusetts, Michigan, Minnesota, Pennsylvania, and Rhode Island have, also passed similar laws aiding the plight of tenants.

Under these laws, the tenant cannot be evicted merely because he lodged complaints against the landlord or engaged in tenant organizing. Moreover, when a tenant vacates an apartment, the landlord must itemize every damage to the vacated apartment before he can deduct any charges from the tenant's

49

deposit or security. If a tenant challenges the landlord's deductions in court and wins, New Jersey law makes the landlord pay double the original security, plus court costs and interest. In New Jersey, tenants also have the right to petition their courts for permission to use their rent to make repairs if their landlord refuses to do so.

In New York City, as of October 1, 1973, for the first time a tenant may petition the new Housing Court of the Civil Court system to remedy a maintenance violation. If the landlord (whether it be a private corporation or even the City of New York) has failed to remedy the violation, the tenant can ask that the landlord be fined. For hazardous violations, a landlord may be fined as much as $100 plus $10 per day until the violation is corrected.

For information about tenants' rights in your state, write to the National Tenant Information Service, 425 13th Street N.W., Washington, D.C. 20005. This agency is an informational clearinghouse that will supply you with the name of the tenant organization nearest you to whom you can write and ask for help in any tenant-landlord problem.

five

Debtor's Property Exempt From Execution

(Property That Cannot Be Taken by the Sheriff or Marshal)

If a creditor does obtain a *judgment* against you, the debtor, he then has to *collect* his judgment. The court cannot order you to pay the money; the court merely gives the creditor his judgment. The creditor then has to have his attorney proceed with various "enforcement proceedings" to collect his judgment. He has to find property from which a Marshal or a Sheriff can collect the amount of the judgment. In order to do this, the creditor, or usually his attorney, makes up an *execution*. The execution is the creditor's command or direction to the Sheriff to proceed against the judgment debtor's property. But by specific laws, certain property is exempt from execution and cannot be touched by the Sheriff or Marshall. The reason for these exemptions is a basic philosophy that the public good takes preference over the individual good; that is, it is thought better to leave the debtor with some property so that he will not be destitute and become a public charge of the state.

However, any exemption provided for by statute is not an automatic exemption. An exemption must not only be *pleaded*, but the debtor must also take some *affirmative action* to take advantage of an exemption. Therefore, you should always consult an attorney when facing a levy against your property.

The laws in the various states differ greatly as to the exemptions a debtor may have. An examination of these laws reveals that some of them are based upon custom and have not been modernized to meet modern-day problems.

For example, in New York State, the Civil Practice Law and Rules, Section 5205(a) exempts the following personal property of a householder from levy and sale by virtue of an execution:

1. Stoves and fuel for 60 days; 1 sewing machine.
2. The family Bible, pictures and school books; books other than the family Bible, not exceeding $50 in value.
3. The family pew in a place of worship.
4. Domestic animals and their food for 60 days, all of which is not to exceed $450 in value.
5. All necessary food actually provided for the use of the judgment debtor or his family for 60 days.
6. All wearing apparel and household furniture, one refrigerator, one radio receiver, crockery, tableware, and cooking utensils necessary for the judgment debtor and the family.

53

7. A wedding ring and a watch, each not exceeding $35 in value.
8. Necessary working tools and implements, including those of a mechanical farm machinery team, as well as professional instruments.
9. "Land set aside as a family or private burial ground that is actually used for that purpose." Such a burial ground must not exceed in extent one-fourth of an acre; and it must not contain at the time of its designation or any time afterwards any building or structure.

New York and most other states allow a householder or head of the family to designate a house and its land as his homestead and exempt part of its value from his general debts. New York's homestead exemption is $2,000; a sample claim for this exemption is presented in Form 3, in the Appendix.

Unlike the archaic New York law, the laws of many other states are generous and realistic in allowing homestead exemptions. In California, a homestead is exempt up to $15,000. In Colorado, $5,000 is exempt from execution. But in many states, including Colorado, the exemption applies only to the head of the family and only if the head of the family records his exemption.

The exemption works this way. Suppose the creditor has a judgment against the debtor for $20,000. Don't laugh. These large judgments can happen especially in the field of personal injury where the debtor's insurance may have lapsed or the debtor was only insured for $10,000 and a judgment of $30,000 was obtained against him. The $20,000 deficiency judgment can be given to the Sheriff in the form of an execution and the Sheriff would levy against the debtor's home. Since in California the first $15,000 is exempt, if the debtor's home was sold for more than $15,000, the debtor would have to be reimbursed from the sale to the extent of $15,000. This would allow the debtor to have sufficient money for a down payment for a new house, if he so desired. However, in those states where an unrealistic sum of $1,000 is the exemption, the debtor would face extreme hardship, especially if he did not file his homestead exemption. In that case, he would get nothing after the sale of his home.

These exemptions seem to discriminate against the average city dweller who has no "homestead."

Other statutes exempt from execution any income received from trusts. A New York statute provides that "any property while held in trust for the judgment debtor where the trust has been created by or the fund so held in trust has proceeded from a person other than the judgment debtor, is exempt from application to the satisfaction of a money judgment." This law, however, does not help a poor person who seldom, if at any time, is a beneficiary of a trust.

In New York a wife's insurance on her husband's life (Domestic Relations Law, Section 52) and payments pursuant to an award in a matrimonial action for support of a wife (Section 5205, C.P.L.R.) are also exempt from execution.

Workmen's compensation and disability benefits are exempt, as are all benefits for injury and sickness disability arising out of and in the course of employment.

Most pensions, especially from governmental agencies, are exempt. In New York benefits from retirement systems and pensions of private firms and corporations may also be exempt under Insurance Law, Section 2007, as are pensions to members of the military services.

Most statutes exempt the "proceeds and avails"—that is, death benefits, cash surrender and loan value, and the dividend —of any insurance policy in which the beneficiary is not the debtor himself. Consequently, in the absence of an intent to defraud creditors, a wife who is a beneficiary under her husband's policy is entitled to the entire insurance fund.

You may wonder why the cash surrender value of the policy is exempt from the claim of creditors. The reasoning is that since the assured has not yet exercised any rights to the proceeds, he has no control over or right to those proceeds. However, it may be that the judgment debtor has assigned his rights to a bank or other third party. Until such bank or third party *exercises* the right, under the assignment, to receive the cash surrender value of the policy, it possesses nothing. Therefore, the attaching creditor, being in np better position than if the assured had not made an assignment, cannot attach those proceeds.

Where the judgment debtor allowed certain dividends on his endowment insurance policy to accumulate interest with the insurance company, the accumulated dividends may be considered proceeds of the policy, and since they, too, go to the

55

beneficiary at the time of the death, accumulated dividends may not be attached.

Most states provide (as the state of New York in its Section 116[3]) that annuities are also exempt.

Benefits of group insurance policies and other annuity contracts, benefits from fraternal benefit societies, and money or benefits from cooperative life and accident insurance companies are entitled to exemption.

Unemployment insurance benefits are exempt. In New York, see the New York Labor Law, Section 595.

Payment to members in military or naval service are exempt from execution.

Veterans' bonuses and all bonuses due servicemen are exempt under Federal law and the law of most states. All benefits to become due under laws administered by the Veterans' Administration are exempt (38 U.S.C.A., Section 3101). Dividend checks from National Service Life Insurance policies, as well as Soldiers' Service Bonds and servicemen's savings are also exempt from execution.

Some other exemptions include:

Shares in savings and loan associations up to $600 (in New York State, under Banking Law, Section 407).

Shares in credit unions up to $600 (in New York State, Banking Law, Section 461).

Pensions of employees of mental institutions (in New York State, Mental and Hygiene Law, Sections 172 and 174).

Teachers' pensions, annuity or retirement allowance benefits (in New York State, Section 524 of the Educational Law).

Compensation paid to recipients of public assistance. Recent interpretation of such law (as New York State Social Welfare Law, Section 137a) has included all recipients of the Medicaid program in New York State as long as the debtor is actually receiving medical care.

Benefits of volunteer firemen (in New York State, Benefit Law 23, Volunteer Firemen Benefits Law).

Accident insurance benefits of volunteer firemen (General Municipal Law 206(b) in New York State).

Interest in the Federal Civil Service Retirement System.

Federal homesteads (43 U.S.C.A., Section 175).

In New York, 90% of personal income, or 90% of income

from trusts as cited above, is exempt from most income executions, (formerly known as garnishees). This means that usually only 10% of a debtor's salary or income may be obtained by the judgment creditor. However, more than 10% of income from these sources may be recovered by the judgment creditor if, by motion (an application to the Court) he can show that the reasonable living requirements of the debtor and his dependents can be met even though larger than 10% payments are made to the judgment creditor.

Some states are much more lenient with the judgment debtors than others. For example, in Texas, salaries and wages are not subject to garnishment at all, and a debtor's home, car, and tools of trade are also exempt from execution. Debtors should acquaint themselves with the exemption statutes of their states by referring to their states' exemption charts.

Later chapters on the enforcement of money judgments will provide more information on this subject.

six

Debtor's Remedies for
Relief From His Debts

BANKRUPTCY

If we go back to the laws of the Twelve Tables (450 B.C.), we find that if a man was indebted to several creditors and couldn't pay his debts, his creditors could actually cut up his body and divide it among themselves. If there was a single creditor, he could put his debtor to death or into slavery. Thankfully, civilization's attitude has changed radically since then; we now treat *deserving debtors* sympathetically. The United States Constitution, for example, specifically provides Congress with the power to establish "uniform laws on the subject of bankruptcy throughout the United States." This provision also means that laws of Congress shall be paramount over insolvency laws passed by any state.

Most states provide by their common law or by statutes, some form of relief for debtors from their debts. This relief usually is the form of "an assignment for the benefit of creditors."

However, it must be noted that only under some form of bankruptcy can the debtor be *completely discharged* from his debts, and because our Constitution gives the Federal government paramount control over bankruptcy, any state statute seeking to grant a debtor complete discharge from his debts would, in all probability, be unconstitutional.

The word "bankrupt" derives from "broken bench" and dates back to the Roman money-changers who set up benches (banks) on which they kept their money. When the money-changer's endeavors failed, his creditors drove him out of business by breaking ("rupting") his bench (bank).

Theoretically, today's bankruptcy laws have two basic purposes. First, to give honest debtors an opportunity to start over again and build a new financial future. Second, to give creditors an opportunity to collect the debtor's assets and share in it equally.

The Federal Bankruptcy Act has 14 chapters. Chapters I through VII deal with "straight" bankruptcy, the most commonly known type.

Chapters VIII, IX, and XII deal with agricultural, railroad, and municipal corporations and with their real property arrangements.

Chapter X deals with corporate reorganization.

61

Chapter XI is used by business people and deals with arrangements with unsecured creditors—that is, creditors who do not hold mortgages or collateral to secure the debt owed to them.

Chapter XII concerns itself with real property arrangements by persons other than corporations.

Chapter XIII deals with "wage earner plans" (discussed in detail later).

Chapter XIV is concerned with Maritime Commission liens.

Since the average man is concerned primarily with Chapters I to VII (straight bankruptcy), Chapter XI (arrangements with unsecured creditors used by business people), and Chapter XIII (arrangements for the wage earner), only those sections will be discussed here.

"Straight" Bankruptcy

"Straight" or personal bankruptcies are steadily increasing. As of this writing, bankruptcies for the past year rose to 182,869, of which personal or "straight" bankruptcies accounted for 90 percent of the total.

When a debtor's liabilities amount to more than the dollar value of his assets, he may put himself into bankruptcy (voluntary bankruptcy) or be "thrown into bankruptcy" by his creditors (involuntary bankruptcy). When a debtor is given a discharge in bankruptcy by the court, without adjudicated objection by a creditor, the debtor's nonexempt assets are collected and distributed on a percentage basis to the creditors listed in his petition according to specified priorities (as set forth at the end of "Straight Bankruptcy"). The remaining portions of the listed debts are thereby discharged, and the debtor is relieved of his obligation to pay them.

It should be noted, however, that it is not necessary for the debtor to be insolvent for him to file a voluntary bankruptcy. There is nothing in the Bankruptcy Law to prevent any debtor from filing a bankruptcy petition, having his assets distributed to pay claims, and having the balance remitted to him.

Many debtors hesitate to go into bankruptcy because they fear that if they do, they won't be able to get any future credit. This fear is largely groundless. In fact, most credit managers would rather give credit to someone recently adjudicated a bankrupt than to someone whose financial condition is not very stable but who has not gone into bankruptcy. The reason is that the law permits a debtor to file for bankruptcy only once every seven years. Therefore, if a person was recently adjudicated a bankrupt, the credit manager need not fear that he will file again to escape paying the new debt.

If you are a harassed debtor, however, you should seriously consider the following questions before filing a petition of bankruptcy:

1. Have you filed a petition in bankruptcy within the past six years?
2. What is the estimated amount you owe to creditors?
3. What is the nature and value of your property? There are various types of "property" which the average person does not consider as "property," but which may be significant in determining whether or not the judgment debtor goes into bankruptcy. For example, consideration should be given to stocks and bonds, including government bonds that may be left in a vault and forgotten about; real property or personal property, possibly located out of the state. Valuable personal property may also include paintings, rare books, jewelry, money owed to you by others, a personal injury action that you may be involved in as a plaintiff and from which you have a contingent or definite amount due you.

   It is to be remembered that an automobile is property as are payments from an insurance company for any fire or theft losses that you may have had.

   You should also consider income tax refunds which have not been received. As to income tax refunds, however, you can send a letter addressed to the District Director of Internal Revenue, directing him to retain any refund and apply it to the taxes presently accruing. If this isn't done, the trustee in bankruptcy will claim any refund due the debtor.
4. Is there a possibility that you will inherit anything within the next six months? If so, the trustee in bankruptcy can claim the inheritance. Such a claim, however, may be legally avoided if it is possible to have the will redrawn and the inheritance left to your children or other relatives.
5. How much of your debt consists of taxes due to the United States government or any state, county, city, or other taxing agency? If the bulk of your debt is taxes, it may be advisable

to arrange payment with the taxing agencies rather than to go into bankruptcy, because *taxes usually are not dischargeable in bankruptcy*. However, if bankruptcy is decided upon, make sure that all taxing authorities concerned know about it and file their claims so that you, the bankrupt, don't have to pay them later.

6. Have you committed any fraudulent act or transfer with respect to any of your money or property? Have you held any property under a fictitious name, or issued any false financial statement to a creditor? Have your turned over any money or property to a creditor, relative, or friend? Do you have any employees whom you owe wages earned within the past three months? Any of the preceding situations may jeopardize discharge of your debts in bankruptcy.

7. If you are in business, what type of business do you have? Certain businessmen such as building contractors cannot readily go into bankruptcy because bankruptcy may result in a temporary or permanent loss of license. It must, therefore, be decided whether bankruptcy will hinder your means of support.

If you do decide to go into "straight" bankruptcy, act quickly. There may be an execution on your income. Upon filing your petitions, however, your attorney can get an immediate stay or restraining order from the Bankruptcy Court to stop the income execution.

Before going into bankruptcy, you should consider whether an individual bankruptcy petition should be filed for your wife or husband, as the case may be, as well as for yourself. During the bankruptcy procedure, it may be possible to get out an order from the Bankruptcy Court to stop creditors from harassing you, the judgment debtor. However, the creditors can and will examine your spouse. If you feel that your spouse "cannot take it," put him or her through bankruptcy as well, especially if your spouse has signed many of the notes or obligations with you.

"Straight" Bankruptcy Procedure

Voluntary bankruptcy is commenced by the debtor's filing of a bankruptcy petition. The petition is a form on which the debtor describes all of his property (assets) and all of his debts (liabilities) and sets forth his exemptions (see Chapter Five). In addition, he sets forth which claims are unsecured, which claims

64

are secured and the types of security involved, and a summary statement of all his debts and assets. Different forms are used for debtors in business and those not in business.

A sample filled-in "straight" bankruptcy petition is presented as Form 4 in the Appendix.

Thus, it is readily seen that unless one is conversant with the law, it would be foolhardy to attempt to institute his own bankruptcy proceedings. An attorney should be consulted.

All bankruptcy matters are handled in the Federal District Courts of the United States and its territories. The petition, in triplicate, is filed with the Clerk of the district in which the debtor has resided or has had his place of business for the six months immediately preceding the filing of the petition.

The mere filing of the petition automatically operates as an adjudication that the debtor is a bankrupt.

After the petition is filed, it is sent to one of the many "Referees in Bankruptcy." The Referee prepares a notice setting forth the final date on which creditors can file their claims and the date on which the first meeting of creditors will be held. This notice is sent to the bankrupt and his attorney and to all the concerned creditors (see Figure 6—1, following).

At the first meeting of creditors, the bankrupt is questioned by the Referee. If the creditors suspect that the bankrupt has hidden assets, they may question him, too. At the meeting the creditors also usually agree to stop all routine collection endeavors. They may also file their claims at that time, although they can wait until the final filing date that had been set by the Referee. A wise creditor files in all cases, even though the debtor's petition shows no assets, because he never knows when hidden assets may be recoverable.

NOTE: If the Bankruptcy Court issues a *restraining notice to creditors,* no further contact with the debtor should be made. If the creditor does contact the debtor directly, he may technically be in contempt of court. Ordinarily, the creditor does contact the debtor in a friendly manner, because if the debtor pays him any part of the debt, the debt may be revived despite the bankruptcy. But the creditor has to be careful that payment to him is not in any way conceived of as a bribe to him to keep him from opposing the bankruptcy.

Figure 6–1

BK-438-S (11–61)

UNITED STATES DISTRICT COURT
FOR THE
EASTERN DISTRICT OF NEW YORK

In the matter of
[Debtor]

in Bankruptcy

Bankrupt.   No.

NOTICE OF FIRST MEETING OF CREDITORS
AND
NOTICE OF ORDER FIXING TIME FOR FILING
OBJECTIONS TO DISCHARGE

(To be used in cases where the filing fees were paid in full at the time of filing)

To the creditors of   [Debtor]

of   [city], N.Y., a bankrupt,

and to other parties in interest:

NOTICE IS HEREBY GIVEN that   [Debtor]

has been duly adjudged a bankrupt on a petition filed by him on   August 21, 1973
and that the first meeting of his creditors will be held at   Room 502, 92–32 Union
Hall St.   in   [city], New York   on   October 3rd, 1973,   at   10:30 o'clock A.M.,
at which place and time the creditors may attend, prove their claims, appoint a trustee, appoint a committee of creditors, examine the bankrupt, and transact such
other business as may properly come before the meeting.

NOTICE IS ALSO HEREBY GIVEN that on the   22nd day   of   September, 1973   an order
was made in the above entitled proceeding, fixing the   14th day   of   November,
1973,   as the last day for the filing of objections to the discharge of the bankrupt.

YOUR ATTENTION is directed to the provisions of the Bankruptcy Act that claims
may not be allowed against the bankrupt estate if not filed within six months after
the first date set for the first meeting of creditors. PROOF OF CLAIM MUST BE
FILED WITH THIS REFEREE AT THE ABOVE ADDRESS whether or not the
debt due the creditor is included in the schedules of the bankrupt. LAST DAY TO
FILE CLAIMS— *April 3, 1974.*

It is essential to the proper administration of bankrupt estates that creditors avoid
giving their proxies to unknown persons who may solicit them. Proxies will not be
recognized by the Referee if it appears that they were solicited in the interest of the
bankrupt or of anyone other than general creditors.

Dated this   22nd   day of SEPTEMBER, 1973   Hon. John Smith
                                                      Referee in Bankruptcy

NOTIFY Referee's office promptly of any change in claimant's post office address.

In cases involving no assets and relatively small debts, the debtor is routinely and briefly examined.

The following is an example of the procedure:

MR. DEBTOR, residing at 110 Main Street, Brooklyn, New York, is sworn in.

EXAMINATION BY THE REFEREE:

Q. Mr. Debtor, are you married or single?
A. Recently divorced.
Q. You reside in an apartment at 110 Main Street, Brooklyn, New York?
A. Yes, since the first of the year. It is not my apartment but under my brother's name and he pays the rent.
Q. Do you pay him a portion of the rent?
A. Yes. I contribute $20 or $25 a week.
Q. What is your business or occupation?
A. I am a butcher for Atlantic and Company.
Q. Where is that located?
A. In Jamaica, Queens.
Q. Is that a wholesale place of business?
A. Manufacturer.
Q. I show you your petition in bankruptcy, your schedule of assets and liabilities and statement of affairs and ask you whether the pages thereof bear your signatures?
A. Yes, sir.
Q. Are they true and correct in all respects?
A. To the best of my knowledge.
Q. Do they list all of your assets and all of your liabilities?
A. Yes, to the best of my knowledge.
Q. In Schedule A2, in your petition in bankruptcy, you list a creditor by the name of ABC Corporation for a refrigerator-freezer for $1,659.30. Was that a commercial freezer or one of these home freezers for delivery with meat and food?
A. It was a food freezer with delivery of meats and groceries.
Q. Have you in the past six years ever been in business in your own name, as a member of a partnership, or as an officer, stockholder, or director of a corporation?
A. No, sir.
Q. What salary do you get?
A. Base salary of $113 a week.
Q. Do you get overtime?

A. If it is busy.

Q. What did you earn last year?

A. Roughly $6,500.

Q. Did you file an income tax return for the year 1972?

A. Not yet.

Q. Will you be entitled to a refund?

A. I wouldn't know, sir.

Q. If you are, I direct that refund be turned over to the trustee who is to be appointed or elected today.

　Do you now own a motor vehicle or have you owned one in the past two years?

A. I have owned one, but I had to turn it in because I was behind in the payments.

Q. When did you return it to the holder of the security?

A. About a month ago.

Q. Was that to the Automobile Acceptance Corporation?

A. Right.

Q. And did you owe them approximately $1,800.50?

A. Yes.

Q. Do you now have a bank account or have you had one in the past two years?

A. When we were married we had one at First National, but it has been closed out for a long time, about four months. There was not much money in there, about $13.

Q. That is what you had in the account at all times?

A. Yes, since we were married.

Q. Have you had a safe deposit box in the last two years?

A. No, never.

THE REFEREE: Are there any creditors present who wish to file claims and nominate or elect a trustee?

ABC CREDITOR'S ATTORNEY: Your honor, I would ask only that a direction be made that the debts listed indicate when they were incurred.

THE REFEREE: I see from the schedules that no dates have been inserted and it is required under the Act. I will direct an affidavit, in duplicate, to be filed within the next 15 days by the bankrupt setting forth, to the best of his knowledge, the dates when these obligations were incurred. Do you wish to nominate a trustee?

ABC CREDITOR'S ATTORNEY: No, your Honor.

THE REFEREE: There being no nominations for trustee, the Court will appoint the trustee during the course of the day. I direct you, Mr. Debtor, to turn over to him all books, rec-

ords, documents, cancelled vouchers, if you have any, bank
statements, and any other papers with regard to your financial
condition. I will adjourn this matter to May 26, 1974 at eleven
o'clock in order to give you an opportunity to file the affidavit
and cooperate with the trustee.

Unless some creditors or the Referee himself has reason for
suspecting that the bankrupt has hidden assets or has committed
some fraud and, therefore, desires further examination, the first
meeting is closed and the bankrupt should receive his discharge
a few months thereafter. A sample order of discharge is presented in Form 5 in the Appendix.

It should be noted that a bankrupt corporation must make
application for a discharge within six months after adjudication.

In cases in which the bankrupt has assets, the Referee will
appoint a trustee (usually an attorney seeking such appointment) to collect assets and, if fraud or concealment of assets is
suspected, to question the bankrupt. The trustee then distributes any assets.

The Federal bankruptcy laws recognize all the exemptions
created by the statutes of the state in which the bankrupt lives.
Therefore, if the bankrupt lives in New York State where the
homestead exemption is now $2,000, this $2,000 of the proceeds from the sale of his homestead must be turned over to
the debtor. The debtor is also protected from execution against
this $2,000 for one year: that is, if an execution against the
debtor's property is issued and the property is sold to satisfy the
execution, $2,000 of the proceeds must be given to the debtor
before the rest of the proceeds go to a creditor.

If the debtor has any assets at all, they are distributed in the
following order or priority:

1. Payment for all costs in preserving the debtor's estate, such
   as putting perishable items in warehouses, and so on.
2. Administrative expenses such as trustee's fees, attorney's fees,
   and cost of stenography minutes.
3. If the bankrupt has employees, their wages and commissions,
   not to exceed $600, due and earned by each employee three
   months before the bankruptcy petition was filed.
4. All taxes due.

69

5. Debts that are entitled to priority in the following order of provable claims:

  (a) Secured claims upon which judgment has been taken.
  (b) Liquidated claims, such as those secured by real estate mortgages and chattel mortgages.
  (c) Other wages of employees.
  (d) Priorities designated by state law.
  (e) Other debts.

Wage Earner's Plan (Chapter XIII of Bankruptcy Act)

It is estimated that over 50 percent of the bankruptcy cases involve wage earners. These wage earners file straight bankruptcy because they are anxious to rid themselves of executions on their salary. Most bankrupts know little about Chapter XIII of the Bankruptcy Act, which is geared to individuals whose principal income is derived from wages.

Chapter XIII provides that either before or after a bankruptcy petition is filed a wage earner may file a petition proposing a plan for the settlement of his debts. The purpose of this plan is to make an arrangement with secured creditors immediately and then to settle unsecured debts to the extent possible. Upon approval of the majority of creditors, the plan is accomplished by submitting future earnings and wages of the debtor to the supervision and control of the Court.

The primary advantage of filing under Chapter XIII for the creditor and the debtor is that they are protected by unforeseen changes in the debtor's circumstances. That protection is available through a provision in Chapter XIII that allows the Bankruptcy Court to modify the amounts to be paid as the debtor's circumstance change.

Because of the ever-increasing number of consumer bankruptcy petitions filed by persons who are heavily in debt and *technically* insolvent, but who evidently are making enough money to pay their present obligations and some of their past obligations as well, some lawmakers want to make it compulsory for wage earners to file under Chapter XIII before proceeding with "straight" bankruptcy. Although the majority of creditors favor this proposal, it can readily be seen that it is most unfair to the wage earner, as he would be deprived of the option of only petitioning for a discharge from his debts through bankruptcy. Thus, such a scheme discriminates against the wage earner in favor of the businessman. Moreover, any such changes to force the wage earner to proceed under Chapter XIII before ordinary bankruptcy would violate the primary purpose of our bankruptcy laws—to enable a debtor to start afresh, relieved from all obligations and bad debts.

Generally, the procedure under Chapter XIII is similar to the "straight" bankruptcy procedure. A debtor files a petition with the Clerk of the District Court (see Form 6 in the Appendix). This petition sets forth the type of property, amount of debts, and the salary earned by the petitioner. It should be noted that when a debtor files a petition under Chapter XIII, he waives all property exemptions that might be available to him under a straight bankruptcy proceeding. The petition is referred to a Referee, who then notifies the creditors (see Form 7 in the Appendix). Meetings of the creditors with the debtor and the Referee are held, and the debtor presents his plan to pay off his debts. A sample of such a plan for payment of debts under Chapter XIII is presented in Form 8 in the Appendix.

If the plan is approved by a majority of the unsecured creditors *and all secured creditors,* the Court then determines whether or not it will approve the plan. If the Court approves, it will appoint a trustee who will supervise and administer the plan to receive monthly allowances from the debtor to pay his creditors. Many plans provide that the debtor's employer deduct a stipulated amount from the debtor's wages and send this amount to the trustee, who then pays the creditors. Other plans provide that the employer sends the trustee the employee's entire paycheck; the trustee allocates to the debtor the balance of the check after payment to the creditors.

The primary advantage to the debtor in Chapter XIII is that the Court may enjoin or stay the commencement of any legal proceeding by the debtor's creditors against the debtor or his property. In addition, the Court may dissolve or stay any garnishee against the debtor's salary and prevent repossession by any conditional seller who may hold a lien on property of the debtor (car, furnishings, appliances, etc.).

The weakness of Chapter XIII from the creditors' point of view is that the plan for payment to current creditors usually does not provide adequate provision for subsequent creditors. Therefore, if the debtor is not properly supervised, he can incur additional debts, making the payment of his present debts hopeless.

From the debtor's point of view, the major problem is the difficulty in qualifying for a wage earner's plan under Chapter XIII, because the debtor must have a good job and sufficient income to make periodic payments of past debts and meet his present debts as well.

Another problem for the debtor is that creditors holding liens on his personal property (e.g., automobile, furniture, etc.) cannot all be treated alike in offering a scaling down of indebtedness or an extension of the time to pay. These secured creditors have to be dealt with individually. Moreover, it is unlikely that a fully secured creditor will consent to anything less than payment in full. Where a secured creditor will not accept the plan, the plan of payment must be altered to exclude that creditor.

Many lawyers would rather put their clients into bankruptcy, and probably rightly so, when one considers the fact that a wage earner's plan may prolong the agony of payment over as long a period as three years. Attorneys argue that it may be better for the nerves of the bankrupt to "get it over with." Further, if the debtor wishes to pay his creditors, even though he has gone through bankruptcy, there is no reason why he could not do so after the bankruptcy.

Following are questions frequently asked about Chapter XIII of the Bankruptcy Act:

1. How does Chapter XIII save me any money? Wouldn't I be better off by consolidating my debts?

ANSWER: There is no interest charged by the Court under Chapter XIII. Nor does the Court charge the high fees that a finance counselor may charge.

2. Must I tell the Court about all my debts or may I hold off those that I want to pay?

ANSWER: You may not hold off those debts that you want to pay. In every bankruptcy situation, the Court must have your entire indebtedness before it; and any trustees appointed must deal with all your creditors.

3. You say that it would take me a long time to get out of debt under Chapter XIII. How long would it take?

ANSWER: Usually arrangements to pay off creditors under

Chapter XIII may take up to three years after the confirmation of a plan by the Bankruptcy Court. However, "if at the expiration of three years after the confirmation of the plan, the debtor has not yet completed his payments thereunder, the Court may nevertheless, upon the application of the debtor, and after a hearing, if it is satisfied that the failure of the debtor to complete his payments was due to circumstances for which he could not be justly held accountable, enter an order discharging the debtor from all his debts and liabilities provided for by the plan, but excluding such debts as are not dischargeable . . . [11 U.S.C., Section 1061]."

4. You say a debtor must file a petition under Chapter XIII. Can you tell us what the petition must state and how a party would go about filing such a petition?

ANSWER: We discussed the filing of a petition above. However, Form 6 in the Appendix will give you an example of a Chapter XIII petition that you could use as a guide should you file without an attorney. But the use of an attorney is always advisable in any court proceedings.

5. What fees are required of me in order to file this petition?

ANSWER: Payment to the Clerk of the Court of $15.

6. Does my employer have to know of my filing under Chapter XIII?

ANSWER: Unless your salary is being garnisheed, your employer need not know of your filing of either a straight bankruptcy petition or a petition under Chapter XIII. Arrangements may be made for you to turn over your salary to a trustee yourself. However, where your salary has already been garnisheed, you may obtain an order from the Bankruptcy Court precluding your employer from turning over any of your salary to the Marshal or the Sheriff until there has been an adjudication under a straight bankruptcy or a release under Chapter XIII.

7. I know that under a straight bankruptcy, I must turn over to the trustee any income tax refund. Does this apply under Chapter XIII?

ANSWER: No, the trustee may request that you return any refund that you receive from income tax, Federal, state or city; but if you need the refund to make payments pursuant to your arrangement with your creditors under this section, you can use those funds to do so.

8. In a "straight" bankruptcy proceeding, the trustee takes

his fee from the top, then the attorneys take their fees, and then the creditors share what is left. Does Chapter XIII usually work the same way?

ANSWER: The trustees under Chapter XIII usually get a moderate fee of only 5%, as one-half of wage earner cases involve $1,000 indebtedness or less and 75% involve $2,000 or less.

9. After I am discharged under Chapter XIII, what kind of credit will I have?

ANSWER: After the completion of this plan, and even after an adjudication under a straight bankruptcy, your credit will be much better than it was prior to your applying for the plan. The reason is that your credit is based upon your ability to pay. Once your debts are discharged—assuming you have the same financial obligations and income as you had previously—your ability to pay will be greater, and hence, so will your credit.

10. Does it make any difference how much my salary or earnings are, in order to qualify for bankruptcy under Chapter XIII?

ANSWER: No, originally this act disqualified petitioners with an income of over $3,600. The figure was raised to $5,000 by subsequent law. But now, all limits have been eliminated.

11. Must all the creditors agree to a plan of payment before the Bankruptcy Court will confirm the plan?

ANSWER: No, only a majority in number of the creditors whose claims have been proved (okayed by the Court) and whose claims represent a majority in dollar amount of claims must accept the plan.

12. Must my plan be in writing and in detail?

ANSWER: Yes, please refer to Form 8 in the Appendix.

13. Can we who are already in bankruptcy ask the Bankruptcy Court to allow us now to file under Chapter XIII?

ANSWER: Yes.

Involuntary Bankruptcy

Involuntary bankruptcy is brought about by the filing of a petition by a creditor against an insolvent debtor with debts over $1,000. Most persons, partnerships, and corporations owing debts can be forced into bankruptcy by their creditors. But the Bankruptcy Act expressly excludes "wage earners" (people earning $1,500 a year or less) and farmers, as well as municipal railroads, insurance and banking corporations.

The main reason that creditors would put a debtor into bankruptcy is to make sure that they have control of the debtor's assets and that there is an equality of distribution. If there has been an assignment for the benefit of creditors, some creditors may suspect that there have been preferential payments or that the debtor is hiding some of his assets. By putting the debtor into involuntary bankruptcy, the creditors can rest assured that they will be given full opportunity to examine the bankrupt in court to determine whether or not there are other assets and what preferential payments have been made, if any. And, if it is found that preferential payments have been made, those payments can be recovered and the creditors can then share in more of the debtor's assets.

Involuntary bankruptcy is instituted by a petition executed in triplicate. A $50 filing fee is paid to the Clerk of the District Court at the time the petition is filed with him.

After the petition is filed, a subpoena is issued by the Clerk of the Court. This subpoena must be served upon the debtor by a United States Marshal within ten days after its issuance. After service upon the alleged bankrupt, he has five days to "plead it." That is, he may answer the petition by claiming that he is not solvent.

If the alleged bankrupt answers that he is insolvent, the matter is put down on the calendar of the United States District Court in the district where the action was brought and a trial with or without a jury will be had. (A jury trial may be demanded by any of the parties.) The questions of fact to be determined at the trial are whether or not the debtor is actually insolvent and whether he committed an act of insolvency (i.e., an assignment for the benefit of creditors) within four months of the date of the filing of the petition. In many instances the parties will agree that matters of fact be determined by a Referee and thereby save time for all concerned.

For all purposes in law, insolvency means that the debtor is unable to meet his debts as they become due, that "his present fair saleable value of assets is less than the amount he will be required to pay on his provable liabilities or his existing debts as they become absolute and mature." Yet our bankruptcy laws have been interpreted to mean that the matter is to be determined strictly by a balance sheet test.

Consequently, it may be very risky for creditors to claim that a debtor is insolvent without making a thorough search of his books, records, and in particular his balance sheet. The reason is that a dismissal of the petition will give the bankrupt the right to sue on the bond which the creditors had to file to assure adequate compensation to the bankrupt should he be wronged (slandered or libeled) by his creditors' petition.

Therefore, when served with a subpoena in an involuntary bankruptcy, debtors should have their attorney check the petition for its contents as well as look into the amount of the bond that was filed. If the bond is not large enough to adequately protect the alleged bankrupt, he can petition the court for an increase in the amount of the bond. Moreover, the alleged bankrupt can sue for an amount in excess of the bond when he has suffered financial damages as a result of the bankruptcy action, and particularly when he can prove that his creditors filed without probable cause and brought their petition maliciously.

Voluntary Arrangements under Chapter XI of the Bankruptcy Act

Any arrangement under Chapter XI of the Bankruptcy Act is a strictly voluntary one. Although it is similar to Chapter XIII, Chapter XI is used by the person in business and its provisions are tailored for him. Only the debtor himself can initiate it. An examination of the petition involved (Form 9 in the Appendix) will show that the debtor acknowledges his insolvent position but offers a proposed plan for payment to his unsecured creditors.

Any debtor (except a banking, municipal, railroad, or insurance corporation, or a building and loan association) can file a petition of arrangement under Chapter XI as a "straight" bankruptcy. The petition is filed in the Federal courts. It may be filed before a bankruptcy action is begun or while an action is pending. The plan of arrangement may classify the unsecured creditors as small and large and propose a payment of 80% of the small debts and 50% of the large debts, the payment to be spread over a two-year period.

As under Chapter XIII, once the petition is filed, the Court may prevent any creditor from commencing or completing a suit against the debtor or from enforcing a lien upon the debtor's property. The Court then offers the petition to a Referee in

Bankruptcy and the Referee calls a creditors' meeting to consider the plan. The creditors are given a copy of the proposed plan along with a copy of the list of the debtor's assets and liabilities. After the creditors file their individual proofs of claims, a creditors' committee is usually appointed to represent all the creditors. The creditors then may propose changes in the debtors' plan, but changes can be made only if the debtor consents to them.

In order for the plan to be put into effect, it must be accepted in writing by a majority of creditors with *proven* claims who represent over 50 percent of the debtor's liabilities. It is to be noted that even though some creditors may object to the plan, if it is accepted by 51 percent of the filing creditors, and the Court approves it, the plan is binding on all creditors, including those who never filed.

When the Court confirms the arrangement, the debtor is discharged from all the unsecured debts covered by the plan.

If a businessman's creditors are stubborn and he can't get a majority of them to agree to a settlement plan, he can turn his settlement petition into a petition for straight bankruptcy. The Court then enters an order declaring the debtor a bankrupt, and proceedings continue as in any other bankruptcy.

Cases in which the debtor still has substantial assets tend to result in out-of-court settlements. Where the assets are not substantial, an assignment for the benefit of creditors may take place. Cases in which the debtor has no assets terminate in bankruptcy.

Where the purpose of the debtor is to remain in business and adjust his obligations, an arrangement under Chapter XI is best.

Reorganizing a Corporation—Chapter X of Bankruptcy Act

Chapter X of the Bankruptcy Act relates primarily to secured debts. Chapter X is used primarily for corporate reorganizations (except for banks, insurance companies, railroads, municipalities, building and loan associations). However, reorganization under this chapter can only be had when adequate relief cannot be obtained by an arrangement under Chapter XI, and the petition must state why proceedings cannot be filed under Chapter XI.

For example, a very large corporation with a large amount of publicly held stock may have a need for a composition agreement with its secured creditors. The importance of whether a corporation files under Chapter X or Chapter XI is that under Chapter XI, management usually remains in control without affecting the rights of secured creditors or the stockholders. Under Chapter X, secured creditors and stockholders have certain additional rights.

A procedure for reorganization under Chapter X may be filed by the corporation itself or by three or more creditors. Once the petition is approved by the Court, creditors, stockholders, bond holders, and the Securities and Exchange Commission must be notified of a hearing to be held "not less than 30 and not more than 60 days" after approval of petition to determine if a temporary trustee is to be appointed.

At the hearing, a trustee is appointed if the debtor's liabilities are $250,000 or more. However, where the assets of the business are less than $250,000, it is discretionary with the Referee as to whether he appoints a Receiver or allows the debtor to continue in business.

Usually various plans for reorganization then **are** submitted by creditors, stockholders, and the trustee. Unlike "straight" bankruptcy and composition proceedings, the number of claimants agreeing with the reorganization plan or with the appointment of a trustee is immaterial. Moreover, when the plan is approved by a majority of the secured creditors and stockholders, its provisions are binding on all involved—including dissenters. But, as in Chapter XI, the failure to finally consummate and get approval of a definite plan may result in an adjudication of bankruptcy.

NON-STATUTORY METHODS OF DEBTOR'S RELIEF

Debt Pooling

Many "debt counsellors" serve the same function as provided for under Chapter XIII of the Bankruptcy Law in that they make arrangements with the creditors for periodic payments from the debtor's salary. Many of these counsellors are sincere and well-intentioned and do a good job. However, as in all other fields of endeavor, some "counsellors" are dishonest, charge excessive fees, embezzle money, and don't pay the creditors. Above all, counsellors cannot stay enforcement of income executions or other proceedings as can the Referee in the Bankruptcy Courts under Chapter XIII. Credit unions and other associations provide "debt pooling" for their members and because they don't charge any fees (fees must be charged in the Bankruptcy Courts), may be advantageous in some cases.

Out-of-Court Settlements: Composition Agreements

Any time a debtor finds that he is financially embarrassed, he can ask his creditors for an extension of time to meet his obligations. Or the debtor can offer a compromise—that is, part payment in full settlement of his account. Settlements are made out of court to save the debtor court costs and fees. The agreements made are contracts between the debtor and creditors whereby the debtor agrees to pay a percentage of the face value of the debt (see Figure 6—2), and the creditors agree to release the debtor from the balance of his debts and forego their other rights against him. This contract is binding on only those who sign it.

Out-of-court settlements do not mean that you have to pay immediately or give your creditor all cash. You may ask your creditor for a moratorium or a delay in payment. (Creditors usually do not grant a delay of more than three years.) You may work out a cash plus post-dated checks settlement, giving the creditor, say, 20% cash and post-dated checks for the months to follow. Or you may work out a settlement with all post-dated checks and no immediate cash. A settlement may be arranged for 50% in cash payable immediately, or 20% cash now and 30% in periodic payments monthly, weekly, or whatever you and your creditor can work out together.

Remember, you have the power to bargain. The creditor knows that by going into bankruptcy, you can wipe out the entire debt. The creditor knows, too, that if he goes to court he has to spend money for an attorney and court costs, as well as additional time in court away from his business. Moreover, it may be bad publicity, especially for a certain type of bank or finance company, to repeatedly go to court.

79

In addition, as we have discussed previously, once the creditor does obtain a judgment against you, he may have difficulty in collecting on it.

If you are a Federal employee, the creditor cannot execute against your wages. If you have assets exempt from execution (as we discussed previously), he cannot grab those assets to satisfy a judgment he may obtain. Even if you have nonexempt assets, it may not be worth his while to follow those assets and execute against them. For example, if you own a car worth approximately $300, it would be foolhardy for your judgment creditor to execute against your automobile. Firstly, the Sheriff or Marshall would be most reluctant to go out and seize such a vehicle; secondly, the cost of doing so and the prospect of receiving only the money gotten through an auction sale would be prohibitive to your creditor.

Therefore, creditors do not take an offer of settlement too lightly; half a loaf is better than none at all. They know that their refusal to grant a debtor's request for an extension of time to make payment or to pay less money may result in the debtor's failure and bankruptcy. Even if the creditor does not accept the offer made, the debtor may sometimes force settlement by petition under Chapter XI or Chapter XIII (later discussed).

When dealing with your creditor, the most important question you will have to answer is whether or not you are sincere and honest in your attempt to settle. You must prove to the creditor that you really haven't any money, or that you have less than he thinks you have, and that you really cannot pay your bills except by composition agreement. If you are in business, it is helpful if you can show your creditor that you probably will be able to continue in business.

Assignment for the Benefit of Creditors

In order to protect the interests of all creditors from the eagerness of some to proceed to judgment and issue executions, debtors, particularly those who have their own businesses, sometimes put their property beyond the reach of any individual creditor. This can be done even when an individual creditor has already obtained a judgment and is threatening to take over the debtor's property by execution.

Figure 6–2

SAMPLE OF ATTEMPT AT OUT-OF-COURT SETTLEMENT

SIDNEY LITIGANT
Attorney-at-Law
(Address)
(Telephone Number)
OR
ALBERT DEBTOR
(Address)
(Telephone Number)

(Date) . . . .

TO: CREDITORS OF ABC CORP.

FROM: ABC Corporation
67 Main Street
Glendale, New York
(zip code)

$623.00
AMOUNT OF CLAIM

Gentlemen:

Because of the recent death of my brother, JOHN DEBTOR, the business conducted by ABC CORP. for over fifty years has steadily declined. In an attempt to preserve and maintain this family business, members of our family have personally invested over $50,000, but to no avail. The business is now discontinued.

The only asset of the company consists of a checking account of approximately $4,000. Much as we would like to pay each creditor in full, this is impossible since the amounts due and outstanding far exceed $6,000. However, we can and do offer to pay to you 25% on each dollar due to you.

If this is agreeable to you, please sign and return to me the enclosed copy of this letter indicating your acceptance. Upon receipt of your acceptance, I shall forward to you a check for the proportionate share due to you in full satisfaction of your claim. The family is willing to disregard its personal loans in an attempt to see that the creditors are satisfied.

Very truly yours,

ABC CORPORATION

By: */s/ ALBERT DEBTOR*
President

One method of stopping the individual creditor and of assuring payments to all creditors is a "general assignment for the benefit of creditors." This assignment is a transfer by a debtor of his property to a third party who is designated a "trustee" and whose role is to apply the property and the proceeds from it to payment of the debts. *The debtor retains no control over his property.* The assignee collects any debts that may be owed to the debtor, sells the debtor's property to the best advantage, and distributes all funds among the creditors on a pro rata basis. The surplus, if any, is returned to the debtor. Forty-two states permit assignments for creditors.

Alaska, Illinois, Maine, Maryland, Nebraska, Nevada, Oregon, and Wyoming have no statutes regulating assignments for creditors. Debtors in those states, therefore, have free rein in making assignments and, aside from fraudulent practices, debtors in those states have full discretion to create all the terms of their assignments. Consequently, they can prefer one creditor over the other, deprive non-preferred creditors of a share of the assets, and give the "trustee" (assignee) broad powers to sell all assets and/or conduct business owned by the debtors.

Many states, however, attempt to prevent abusive treatment of creditors through statutes that regulate assignments for the benefit of creditors. These statutes are so different from one another that comparisons cannot easily be made. For example, Idaho's statute simply provides that an assignment is valid if the assignee is a resident of Idaho. Georgia's statute provides for only partial assignment.

Under most statutes, however, consent of two-thirds of a debtor's creditors is necessary for an assignment to take place. Some states, including New York, have complex statutes; the more complex the statute, the more complicated the procedure.

Ordinarily, the practical effect of an assignment would be to put the debtor's property beyond the reach of the Bankruptcy Court. The Bankruptcy Law, therefore, provides that an *assignment for the benefit of creditors is an act of bankruptcy if made within four months preceding the filing of a petition of bankruptcy.*

A decree of bankruptcy sets aside an assignment for the benefit of creditors. Therefore, if some of the creditors feel that the assignment is not in their best interest, they can force the debtor into bankruptcy.

82

Credit management associations and creditors in general seem to prefer assignments as a means of liquidation of insolvent estates. The reason is that this method gives creditors the opportunity to examine the debtor's books, look into the conduct of the debtor's business, and ascertain the debtor's motives. Then, if the creditors are not satisfied with what they find, they can push the debtor into involuntary bankruptcy. On the other hand, if they are satisfied, they have some control over the debtor's property because a member of the credit association or its lawyer or one of the creditors is usually appointed as the assignee.

Let us assess the advantages and disadvantages of an assignment for the benefit of creditors.

Advantages to Debtor
1. An assignment can be used where a debtor cannot get a discharge in bankruptcy.
2. All the formal hearings and subjection to the Bankruptcy Court are avoided. Moreover, an assignment eliminates the cost of filing for bankruptcy, stenographic fees, and the fees accorded to a trustee in bankruptcy.
3. Adverse publicity may be avoided. Bankruptcies are regularly published in various law journals and periodicals, as well as in daily newspapers. Assignments for the benefit of creditors, on the other hand, may be known only to those creditors who are consulted.
4. Creditors favor assignment because they may get more money than they would through the debtor's bankruptcy. More funds are available because the assignee has a greater opportunity to sell the debtor's assets to the highest bidder.
5. Property transferred to a third party, such as an assignee, is not subject to attachment by creditors as it is in a bankruptcy action.

Disadvantages to Debtor
1. An assignment for the benefit of creditors is an act of bankruptcy, and any individual creditor can take the matter out of the hands of the assignee and other creditors by filing a petition of bankruptcy against the debtor.
2. In a bankruptcy proceeding, acts of the debtor can be freely explained during his examination. There is no such procedure for an assignment.

83

3. The debtor cannot get a discharge from his debts.
4. Because of the lack of uniformity among state courts, assignments have limited territorial jurisdiction.

Advantages to Creditors
1. Only those creditors who give their consent to an assignment procedure are bound by the assignment. Therefore, unless it is possible to get the agreement of all the major creditors and a great number of those with smaller claims, it doesn't pay to go into an assignment.
2. Any creditor who does not agree with the assignment can just sit back and wait until the debtor has acquired new assets and then proceed to judgment and execution on those new assets.
3. In a bankruptcy proceeding a trustee, who is under the jurisdiction of the Bankruptcy Court, may be appointed to retain the property of the debtor. Under an assignment, the assignee is usually a representative of the creditors and he can handle the debtor's property as the creditor desires without having to receive permission from the Court.

Assignment for Benefit of Creditors Procedure

In those states where assignment for benefit of creditors is codified by statute, the procedure is more complex than it is where there are no such statutes.

In the case of statutory assignments the procedure is as follows:

The written assignment lists and describes all the property transferred to the assignee and designates the creditors for whose benefits the assets have been assigned.

An assignment is executed (signed and sworn to) by the assignor (debtor) and, in some states, by the assignee after the assignment is recorded in the County Clerk's office. Form 10 in the Appendix presents a sample of a general assignment.

The assignment is then delivered to the assignee along with all property listed in the assignment.

The assignee must then file a bond to secure the faithful performance of his trust.

Next, the assignee gives public notice to all creditors listed, and the creditors are asked to file their claims with the assignee.

Debtors of the assignor/debtor are asked to pay all their debts to the assignee. The assignee then goes about collecting the assignor's debts and distributing the assignor's assets. If the assignor has a business, the assignee may actually run the assignor's business during this period. However, the business is usually continued only in order to complete business matters.

Usually the assignee's most important function is the disposal of the assignor's assets by sale. In selling the goods assigned to him, the assignee must be careful he does so with prudence. He must provide adequate insurance and protect the goods; he must not delay his sale too long; he must sell at a reasonable price and account for all goods sold.

After deducting all expenses, including his own compensation, the assignee makes payment to the creditors according to priorities. Any surplus remaining is paid to the assignor. All of the assignee's accounts are examined by the Court and a final accounting must be filed by the assignee and approved by the Court. Upon approval by the Court, and after a reasonable time, the assignor is relieved from his bond.

EXAMPLES OF STATE LAWS THAT CAN BE USED FOR DEBTOR'S RELIEF

New York's Business Corporation Law

Article X of New York's Business Corporation Law is an example of a state law that can be used for corporate debtor relief. Under Article X, a corporation may be dissolved by consent of two-thirds of the stockholders. Notice must then be given to the creditors to file their claims. Creditors who file their claims have the right to have their cases heard in the Supreme Court or the Superior Court where the petition for dissolution was filed. Once it is dissolved, the corporation is relieved of all liability to creditors who received notice but failed to bring suit against the corporation or file objections to its dissolution. Those creditors are barred from participating in the distribution of assets.

This statute is used to best advantage in a situation where a corporate debtor wants no stigma of an assignment and no court controls or delay-causing orders. Under this statute a corporation with a large inventory can retain control of it, sell it quickly, and then dissolve. Of course, this procedure works well only where the corporation has no problems with its creditors.

Remember also that under this statute no discharge from debts is given. Moreover, if a corporation has a lease that still has a long term to run, the corporation is responsible for the entire loss incurred by the landlord—not only for the loss for one year as under straight bankruptcy or assignment statutes.

Community Property Laws

By moving into a state where community property is respected, a harassed debtor may be safe from the clutches of his attaching creditors.

By community property we mean that all property acquired by either husband or wife after the marriage is deemed to be the result of the joint effort of both husband and wife and therefore belongs to both of them. This definition does not apply to inheritances or gifts as long as such assets are kept in a separate fund. But all earnings of the husband and wife after marriage are deemed community property in a community property state.

Consequently, if a husband or his wife is deeply indebted in New York, the husband and wife can move to California (a community property state), maintain residence, start a bank account, and thumb their noses at *past* creditors. The new community property bank account, as well as their possessions, will be free from the husband's or wife's individual past debts. For example, if a wife had a judgment against her before her marriage, the savings account she now maintains with her husband cannot be seized so long as she remains married.

Once a husband and wife establish residence under community property law, the husband has the right to manage and control the community property and hence (except in the state of Washington) he can sell and mortgage any community property without his wife's consent. But the community property cannot be encumbered or be attached for a debt incurred by the husband if both husband and wife do not benefit from the debt. For example, community property cannot be attached for a husband's $500 golf club purchase or for his debts in "doing the town" with his cronies.

The theory of community property law originated with the French and Spanish "Civil Law" as distinguished from the

86

"Common Law" of English derivation. Consequently, states founded by the French or Spanish colonists usually maintain community property laws. These community property states include Louisiana, Texas, California, Nevada, Arizona, Washington, Idaho, Montana, and New Mexico.

seven

Actions Against a Debtor
After Bankruptcy or Judgment

CREDITORS' SUIT ON A DEBT EVEN AFTER BANKRUPTCY

Most debtors believe that once they have initiated bankruptcy proceedings, filed a schedule, and paid a filing fee, they no longer have to worry about their creditors. Consequently, when served with a summons after they have filed bankruptcy proceedings, they simply ignore the summons.

Many debtors believe, too, that once bankruptcy is filed a summons that was served and filed prior to the bankruptcy will have no effect upon them.

Moreover, many debtors have the illusion that once they are discharged, their bankruptcy wipes out all those debts listed in the schedule of the bankruptcy proceeding.

The facts are that the right to discharge the debts listed in the schedule of bankruptcy is determined by the Referee in Bankruptcy. The effect of this discharge on each particular debt is determined by the state court. Thus, the bankruptcy proceeding only wipes out debts that are dischargeable.

However, a creditor still may bring an action on one of these very same debts, and it is incumbent upon the debtor in such an action in court to plead as his defense that the debt being sued on has been discharged in the bankruptcy proceeding.

To make this matter clearer, we can refer to the analogous situation of a contract made by an infant (that is, a minor, who in most states is anyone under 21 years of age).

Infant *A*, 18 years of age, purchased a television set on time. After making two payments, *A* defaulted on further payments, and the creditor sued for the balance of the money. Since a television set is a luxury item, and an infant is not responsible for contracts for other than items of necessity under certain conditions, *A* can avoid his contract by claiming that he was an infant at the time of the sale.

However, if *A* doesn't answer the summons and doesn't let the court know that he has the defense of infancy, his defense is of no use to him. Therefore, unless *A* actually pleads in court, the creditor will obtain a judgment against him.

The same situation exists as to the bankrupt. Unless the bankrupt pleads his bankruptcy, there is no way that the court would know that the bankrupt wishes to avoid the payment of this particular debt because of his bankruptcy. Therefore, unless he

91

uses this "affirmative defense" of bankruptcy, judgment will be obtained against the bankrupt and execution on his remaining assets or income will be issued.

The obvious lesson to be learned is that the bankrupt should *immediately* forward to his attorney any summons or other court process received by him *prior to* and *after* he institutes bankruptcy proceedings. If the bankrupt neglects doing so and judgment against him is entered and execution is commenced, he will be forced to spend more money in an attempt to vacate the judgment and the execution pending against him.

RELIEF FROM JUDGMENT AFTER BANKRUPTCY

If the bankrupt has been negligent and judgment has been entered, it may be possible under state law to set aside the judgment because of "mistake, inadvertency, or excusable neglect."

If the judgment against the bankrupt has been filed before the bankrupt has been discharged, the best practice is for the bankrupt individually or through his attorney to plead the adjudication of bankruptcy and ask for a stay of execution until the discharge is granted; after discharge, the bankrupt must plead the affirmative defense of bankruptcy against the judgment that had been entered.

If the debtor-bankrupt has delayed pleading this affirmative defense, he has the additional remedy of going into the Bankruptcy Court and asking for an order restraining his creditors in their suit in the state court. It is well established in law that the Bankruptcy Court has jurisdiction to enjoin a state court from proceeding in a case such as this.

It must be noted with great emphasis, however, that non-scheduled creditors (those creditors not listed in the petition of the bankrupt) are not discharged and can sue in the state court. The debtor's remedy in such a situation is to prove, if he can, that those creditors had actual notice of the bankruptcy proceeding.

PROCEEDING AGAINST THE BANKRUPT DEBTOR

After the debtor has already been discharged in bankruptcy, the judgment creditor may be able to proceed against the debtor, even though his specific claim had been "discharged." This is especially so if the debtor had made a "fraudulent" statement to his creditor about his assets. Although such a fraudulent statement made by one not in business will not be sufficient to block a discharge in bankruptcy, the creditor can proceed in the state court on his original claim. Thus, if the bankrupt debtor is not a businessman, the creditor's summons and complaint in the state court will be an action based upon fraud. If the creditor can show that he was defrauded, the debtor's answer that bankruptcy has wiped out his creditor's claim will be of no avail.

FRAUDULENT TRANSFERS—BADGES OF FRAUD

The problem in the collection of judgments resolves itself mainly in the various procedures of investigation for the purpose of locating the judgment debtor and his assets. When a debtor transfers rather than conceals his assets, the creditor has an entirely different task. The subject of transfers (conveyances) that are fraudulent is a large one and cannot be fully explored here. However, it is imperative that the debtor knows that there are laws designed to protect the creditor from a debtor's fraudulent transfers. If he does not realize that, the debtor may not only be lulled into a sense of false security but also perpetrate additional fraudulent transfers.

Under controlling statutes, mainly the Uniform Fraudulent Conveyance Act and, in New York, Article X of the Debtor and Creditor Law, a fraudulent conveyance is defined as a conveyance made or an obligation incurred—without regard to the conveyor's intent—for which the conveyor has not received a fair consideration but which renders him insolvent. In addition, a fraudulent conveyance may be an obligation incurred or conveyance made with intent to hinder, delay, or defraud creditors.

BULK TRANSFERS

By the common use of the term "bulk transfer" we mean the sale of a substantial portion of a business's fixtures, stock, and trade. The debtor businessman must be careful to note that

93

statutes have been designed to prevent the defrauding of his judgment creditors by the *secret* sale of such assets. If the judgment debtor does secretly make bulk transfers, his judgment creditors can bring suit against him again.

eight

*What Debtors Should
Know About How Creditors
Collect Their Judgments*

It is our aim in this chapter merely to acquaint you with some of the procedures that creditors take for the enforcement of their money judgments; that is, in order to reduce the judgment (or decision of the court) into money for themselves.

In enforcing their judgments, creditors have three basic goals:

1. To locate the judgment debtor or his assets.
2. To assure that the assets once located are not removed or transferred to some other party, in order to be out of reach of the judgment creditor.
3. To transfer the assets of the judgment debtor to the judgment creditor.

We shall take a look at each of these basic goals for the purpose of understanding the various procedures used by the creditors.

HOW CREDITORS USE THE LAW TO LOCATE THE DEBTOR OR HIS ASSETS

Various laws give the creditor the right to subpoena in order to locate the debtor or the debtor's assets. To learn the location of the debtor or the debtor's assets, the creditor can subpoena the debtor's spouse, the debtor's relatives, friends, or business associates. In order to obtain assets of the judgment debtor, the debtor himself may be subpoenaed.

In New York State, a person may be subpoenaed by certified or registered mail. This is known as an "information subpoena," which includes questions for the debtor to answer and a prepaid return envelope (see Form 11 in the Appendix for examples of the types of questions asked). Answers must be made in writing, under oath, by the person upon whom the subpoena is served and must be returned within seven days after receipt of the subpoena. If the debtor or other party subpoenaed does not return the subpoena, the judgment creditor can then issue a subpoena requiring the debtor's attendance for the taking of a deposition.

In an examination of a debtor, the creditor's attorney may try to make the debtor believe that the attorney for the creditor knows nothing about the debtor's assets and that he believes

97

everything that the debtor tells him. The creditor's attorney may thus obtain from the debtor certain information on the "Q.T." Be careful of this tactic. Further investigation may lead the creditor to assets that the debtor did not wish to discuss.

The spouse of the judgment debtor can and is often subpoenaed by serving her with a "witness subpoena." The creditor knows that mere service upon the debtor's spouse may create enough dissension and argument in the home to result in speedy payment of the debt.

HOW CREDITORS USE CONTEMPT PROCEEDINGS AGAINST DEBTORS

If the judgment debtor or a witness does not answer or comply with any of the subpoenas or restraining notices hereinafter discussed, an "order" is then served upon the errant judgment debtor or third party requiring him to show cause why he should not be cited for contempt of court.

Failure to comply with or to answer the "order to show cause" will usually result in a "bailable attachment" order being issued by the judge. The latter order authorizes the Sheriff's deputy to actually go out and bring the debtor bodily before the court. Since the debtor is in contempt of court, the judge may fine the debtor (usually in the amount of the judgment) and have the fine turned over to the creditor, or he may order the debtor imprisoned.

HOW CREDITORS GET INFORMATION ABOUT DEBTORS

Information from Banks

Under most collection statutes, there is no separate provision for obtaining information from banks. However, an "information subpoena" can be served upon banks to obtain information about a judgment debtor.

If the judgment creditor knows where the debtor banks, an execution to the Sheriff can be made immediately. This has a twofold purpose: firstly, it ties up the bank account; secondly, it puts the creditor in a position to obtain this money from the bank by a levy. However, if the creditor does not know in what bank the debtor keeps his money, the creditor can, under most statutes, go on a "fishing expedition" by sending an information subpoena to all banks that the judgment creditor believes may have an account for the debtor. Along with the information subpoena, the creditor usually includes a restraining notice. If one of the banks has an account for the debtor, the restraining notice will stop the bank from making payments to him.

A sample of an information subpoena with restraining notice is presented in Form 12 in the Appendix.

Information from Other Parties

Various other kinds of information concerning the judgment debtor and his assets may be obtained from others with whom the debtor is doing or has done business. For example, subpoenas, either information subpoena or actual service of subpoena for examination, may be made on various utilities who may have credit information that would be helpful to the creditor. Valuable information may be received from utilities as to the name and address under which service had been given, as well as credit information given to the utilities at the time the debtor's account was opened.

LEGAL STEPS CREDITORS TAKE AGAINST DEBTORS

The Restraining Notice

Once the debtor's address is ascertained, the creditor can serve the debtor with a restraining notice. Immediately upon being served with a restraining notice the debtor cannot, under most statutes, sell, assign, transfer, or interfere with any property in which he has an interest, except pursuant to direction of the Sheriff or pursuant to a court order,* until the judgment involved is satisfied or vacated.

A restraining notice served upon a third party has the same effect *only if at the time of the service* the third party owes a debt to the debtor or has in his possession or custody property which

---

* A restraining notice does not prohibit the debtor from spending his earnings.

he *knows or has reason to believe* the debtor has an interest in.

The powers of this restraining notice may go further than the mere notice indicates. It has been held in some states that a restraining order served on a judgment debtor is effective to prohibit the debtor from transferring property acquired after he receives the notice.

Disobedience of the restraining notice is punishable, as is the disobedience of a subpoena, by a contempt of court citation.

One of the most effective ways of restraining the debtor is the docketing (filing) of the money judgment or the transcript of a money judgment in the county where the judgment debtor has real property. The mere docketing of a judgment in that county will, in essence, prevent the judgment debtor from selling or transferring that property.

Sheriff's Levy

A levy by the Sheriff against the property of the judgment debtor or against a garnishee third party restrains the judgment debtor or the third party, as the case may be, from disposing of any of the property so levied upon. In fact, the judgment creditor may serve an execution instead of serving a restraining notice upon the judgment debtor or third party. In this way, the judgment creditor can stay transfer of any property that would also be attachable and subject to the Sheriff's execution—even property the creditor may not have anticipated that the judgment debtor or third party garnishee had in his possession.

Execution to Sheriff or Marshal

In areas that have city marshals an execution may be given to a City Marshal or to a Sheriff. The City Marshal is appointed by the Mayor; it is usually a political "patronage" job.

A levy by the Sheriff upon real property is not necessary because the judgment or transcript of the judgment may be docketed in the county where the property is located; that itself gives the judgment creditor a lien on this property.

Since most people drive automobiles today, an execution is usually made against the judgment debtor's vehicle. However, before issuing an execution to a Marshal or Sheriff to pick up the judgment debtor's automobile, a search is made to de-

100

termine whether or not there are any mortgages on the car. Such a search may reveal the name of a bank or finance company from which other information about the assets of the judgment debtor may be obtained.

However, an execution to the Sheriff or Marshal giving him the registration number and further description of the automobile will not always bring results. A Sheriff or Marshal usually will not go out in the early hours of a morning when an execution against an automobile should be made. There are private detectives who specialize in repossessing vehicles. When they locate a vehicle they work closely with the Marshal or Sheriff who makes the levy. After the car is "picked up," the police department is notified, so the repossessor is not arrested for "stealing" a reported stolen car.

But the debtor should know that a Sheriff, Marshal, or repossession agent has no right to go upon private property or to use unnecessary force in executing upon an automobile—or upon any property.

After an execution is made, the Marshal or Sheriff usually puts the property up for sale. But a sale may be postponed from time to time, especially if the judgment creditor stands to gain more by getting some money periodically from the judgment debtor than by proceeding by sale. Form 13 in the Appendix presents a sample announcement of a sheriff's sale.

Income Execution (Formerly Called Garnishee)

If the judgment debtor is regularly employed, the judgment creditor can seek an income execution similar to the sample shown in Form 14 in the Appendix. Under the old laws, especially in New York State, it was necessary to first issue an execution against the property of the judgment debtor before one could proceed against the debtor's salary. Now the creditor can immediately execute against the judgment debtor's income.

But the Federal law limits the amount of "earnings" that the employer can take from his worker. By the term "earnings" the Federal law means compensation paid or payable for personal services, whether called wages, salary, commission bonus, or otherwise. Although various state laws provide that an employer can take more than 25% of "earnings per week, the *federal* law *controls,* and it generally limits the maximum garnishment of any worker's salary to 1.25% of the disposable earnings per week. "Disposable earnings" means that part of earnings that remain after deductions required by law. (Such deductions are Federal income tax withholding deductions, Federal Social Security tax deductions, city and state withholding taxes and income taxes.)

As an alternative to the 1.25% weekly maximum, the Federal law allows for garnishment of the amount of weekly disposable earnings that exceeds 30 times the Federal minimum hourly wage in effect at the time earnings are payable.

However, in accordance with the Federal law, an employee's earnings in any given week may not be garnisheed at all if his disposable earnings are $48 or less.

It is also to be noted that in many states the employee's salary cannot be garnisheed unless the employee makes at least $85 per week. (See Exhibit 3 in the Appendix for garnishee requirements of each state.)

The Federal law restricting wage garnishments has other provisions. For example, the law prohibits any employer from discharging an employee because his earnings have been garnisheed for any "one indebtedness"—regardless of the number of creditors seeking satisfaction by means of the garnishment.

Installment Payment Order

When the judgment debtor is self-employed, or has an income from a trust fund or an income from some enterprise that the judgment creditor can't exactly put his finger on, or if the judgment debtor is employed out of the state but lives within it, or if he is "employed" in his wife's business, the judgment creditor will usually "run the gamut" to bring the debtor in for examination. The reason for this is that, based on the information the creditor obtains at an examination, the creditor can ask the Court for an order requiring the debtor to pay specified amounts in installments to the creditor. This application for an order is also used if the debtor will receive money from any source or is attempting to impede the creditor by rendering personal service without adequate pay.

102

HOW A CREDITOR CAN LEGALLY USE A RECEIVER

Another one of the effective ways the creditor may obtain possession of the debtor's assets is through the appointment of a receiver of the property of the debtor, excluding exempt property and salary. A receiver may be empowered to negotiate a sale of this property. The appointment of a receiver is especially used when the debtor is operating a business or owns other income-producing property.

The law provides for the appointment of only one receiver of the debtor's property. Once this receiver has been appointed, a creditor can petition the court (by motion brought on by "Order to show cause") to extend the receivership.

Another, although rarely used, remedy of the creditor is the "order of arrest," previously known as a "body execution." "Body execution" as an enforcement of judgment tool for the creditor was abolished by statute in New York State. However, where the debtor is so concealing himself or is about to flee from the state so that it is impossible to serve a subpoena or notice upon him the New York law provides for an Order of Arrest.

When the debtor is brought into court after being arrested by the Sheriff, the Court may ask him to put up a bond before he will be released. This bond will secure the creditor and make collection of the judgment feasible.

TRANSFERRING THE DEBTOR'S ASSETS FOR CREDITOR'S BENEFIT

Where the debtor has in his possession or custody money or other personal property, the judgment creditor may ask the Court to direct the debtor to turn over to the judgment creditor such money or property he has as will be sufficient to satisfy the amount of the judgment of the creditor.

In one case based on negligence action, a judgment was obtained against Mr. X for over $180,000, with only $25,000 insurance coverage. Mr. X, however, had large stock interests in multiple family corporations. After serving subpoenas on those corporations and obtaining affidavits from them regarding Mr.

X's stock interests, the creditor proceeded by motion to have these stocks transferred to the Sheriff and sold at auction. Needless to say, however, before the sale, a satisfactory settlement of the judgment was arranged by the family corporations. No doubt the corporations did not relish the thought of possible control of their business by strangers.

SPECIAL WAYS CONTRACTORS AND MATERIALMEN CAN LEGALLY COLLECT FROM DEBTORS

Most states protect contractors, subcontractors, and materialmen by giving them liens on the property on which they work. The reason for this special protection is that the materialman, workman, or contractor has added to the value of the property and because his material has become part of the property he cannot take it back.

Furthermore, many states also help contractors and materialmen by providing that funds held by any person pursuant to an agreement made in a deed, mortgage, or other instrument shall be trust funds in the hands of such person to be applied first for the payment to contractors and materialmen who worked on that property. A violation of this law gives the materialman or workman the right to seek criminal or civil relief.

nine

*If the Creditor Does Not
Collect with Care
You May Have
an Action Against Him*

The judgment creditor must collect with care. Unless he does so, he may be subject to charges based on assault or battery, libel, slander, violation of postal regulations, extortion, and, in some jurisdictions, invasion of the right of privacy.

ASSAULT OR BATTERY

An assault may be defined as an attempt, with unlawful force, to inflict bodily injury upon another, accompanied by an apparent present ability to give effect to the attempt if not prevented. There must be some overt act or threatening gesture. Words alone never amount to an assault.

Remember, however, that a debtor may also be guilty of an assault. For example, a debtor who shuts a door on his creditor with sudden violence for the purpose of striking the creditor has committed an assault.

A battery is the intentional commission of physical harm. Therefore, an assault (an attempt to harm) which is successful is a battery. It is generally said that a battery consists of a physical injury actually done in an angry, vengeful, or rude manner.

LIBEL OR SLANDER

A libel consists of the communication of false, defamatory matter in a permanent form, such as a writing, print, painting, a piece of statuary, or even a phonograph record.

Slander is the communication of false defamatory matter which is not in permanent form, such as that circulated by word of mouth.

By defamation we mean damage to the reputation of a living person by causing that person to be shunned, ridiculed, hated, or held in contempt by his community at large. However, for libel or slander to be committed, the matter communicated must be both public, that is, someone other than the debtor must have heard or seen the defamation, and intentionally defamatory.

But it must be noted that truth is an "absolute defense" against libel and slander. Therefore, if your creditor communicates something about you—no matter how defamatory or widely public—you will lose in a lawsuit against him if the matter communicated is true.

107

Consequently, a debtor can make a good cause of action against his creditor who has *falsely* accused him in front of his neighbors of being a "drunken dead beat." So, too, a creditor who falsely informed a neighbor that the debtor was in extreme delinquency on his debts can be sued for slander.

INVASION OF THE RIGHT OF PRIVACY

If the creditor uses unreasonable harassing collection tactics or unreasonably frightens a layman with "deliberately prepared documents" that look like court processes to which the creditor may not be entitled under the law, the debtor may have a right of action for invasion of his right of privacy. But not all states recognize invasion of privacy as a cause for a lawsuit. In those states that do recognize it, the facts in each case determine whether or not the creditor has "unduly harassed" the debtor in an attempt to collect his debt. Moreover, the debtor has to prove his damages and show what he has lost as a result of the creditor's actions.

The modern trend to protect the consumer has resulted in some successful actions against creditors who have given credit information (obtained from their customers) to various credit bureaus. Therefore, creditors seek to protect themselves from any possible future legal actions by adding the following paragraph into their credit application:

> I duly authorize and give to creditor, his agents, servants or employees, full access and permission to investigate my past and present background in order to obtain knowledge of my financial responsibility.

"Agents" here may refer to credit bureaus used by creditors. So look for this paragraph in your next credit application before you sign and, if you can, go elsewhere and buy your merchandise at the same price and credit without signing an application with that kind of clause.

VIOLATION OF POSTAL REGULATIONS

It is interesting to note that the creditor must also be cautious that he does not violate any of the postal regulations in dealing with the debtor or in his attempt to locate a debtor. For example, a creditor may send a gimmick postcard or letter to the debtor with the heading "Government Identification Service," or something of the sort, asking the debtor to fill in his name, address, place of work, and so on and return it to the sender. The debtor may think he's providing the information to some official agency, whereas he's really giving the creditor facts he wants. It is to be noted that violation of any postal regulation may result in the creditor being fined or even imprisoned!

EXTORTION

In trying to collect his debt, a creditor may commit extortion by threatening the debtor so as to induce fear in him of extreme consequences if he does not pay. For example, the Penal Law of the State of New York defines extortion in this way: "Fear, such as will constitute extortion, may be induced by an oral or written threat: (1) to do an unlawful injury to the person or property of the individual threatened, or to any relative of his or any member of his family, or to a corporation of which he shall be an officer, stockholder, employee or agent; or (2) to accuse him or any relative of his or any relative of his family of a crime; or (3) to expose or impute to him or any of them any deformity or disgrace. . . ."

It is especially to be noted that it is unlawful for the creditor to threaten any *criminal action* for nonpayment of a debt. Payment of a debt is purely a civil liability and has nothing to do with our criminal courts unless some criminal fraud is involved.

Appendix

EXHIBITS AND SAMPLE FORMS

Exhibit 1   Interest Chart

Each state has its own laws regarding the rates of interest that may be charged on various loans. If the lender takes from the buyer interest greater than that allowed by law, he may be subject to various penalties. Some states provide that if a creditor charges usurious interest (that is, interest over the amount allowed by law in that particular state), he may not recover any interest at all; other states provide that when usurious interest is received by the creditor, the creditor forfeits double or even triple the amount of interest taken. Many states provide that the charging of exorbitant interest is a crime.

The following chart sets forth the rates of interest in accordance with the laws of the various states. Interest rates are changing daily. Therefore, this chart can be merely a guide.

STATE	LEGAL RATE	CONTRACT RATE	CORPORATE RATE	PENALTY
ALABAMA	6%	8%	8% to $10,000 15% $10,000 to $100,000 No limit on excess	Forfeit all interest
ALASKA	6%	8%	No limit	Forfeit all interest
ARIZONA	6%	10%	1½% per month if debt is over $5,000	Forfeit all interest
ARKANSAS	6%	10%	No statutory provision	Contract is void
CALIFORNIA	7%	10%	No provision	Forfeit all interest (Charging usurious interest is a misdemeanor.)
CONNECTICUT	6%	12%	18% if debt is over $10,000	Forfeit all interest and principal (Charging usurious interest is a misdemeanor.)
COLORADO	6%	45% and as limited by U.C.C.	No statutory provision	No statutory provision
DELAWARE	6%	~9%	No usury defense	Forfeit excess over 6%
DISTRICT OF COLUMBIA	6%	8%	Unlimited	Forfeit all interest

112

STATE	LEGAL RATE	CONTRACT RATE	CORPORATE RATE	PENALTY
FLORIDA	6%	10%	15%	Forfeit all interest and forfeit interest and principal if interest is over 25% (Charging usurious interest is a misdemeanor.)
GEORGIA	7%	8%	Unlimited on loans of $2,500 or more	Forfeit all interest
HAWAII	6%	12%	No statutory provision	Forfeit all interest (Charging usurious interest is a misdemeanor.)
IDAHO	6%	10%	17% on loans over $10,000	Three times interest charged
ILLINOIS	5%	8% Business or corporate loans any rate	Unlimited	Forfeit all interest, plus penalty of 2X interest paid in two years (Charging of usurious interest is a misdemeanor.)
INDIANA	8%	8%	Unlimited	Forfeit interest over 8% or 10X excess charged if refund refused
IOWA	5%	9%	Unlimited	Forfeit all interest and 8% of unpaid principal, plus pay equal sum for county school fund
KANSAS	6%	10%	No usury defense	Double the excess over legal rate
KENTUCKY	6%	8½%	No usury defense	Forfeit all interest and return interest paid within two years (Charging usurious interest is a misdemeanor.)
LOUISIANA	7%	8%	Unlimited	Forfeit all interest and return interest paid within two years

STATE	LEGAL RATE	CONTRACT RATE	CORPORATE RATE	PENALTY
MAINE	6%	None (for nonbusiness loans)	No statutory provision	Personal loans made after $2,000, judgment void and pay attorneys' fees
MARYLAND	6%	6%	No usury defense	Forfeit 3X interest or $2,500, whichever greater
MASSACHUSETTS	6%	Unlimited	Unlimited	
MICHIGAN	5%	7%	Unlimited	Forfeit all interest, pay court costs and attorneys' fees
MINNESOTA	6%	8%	None	Contract void; repay interest within two years after paid if over 20%
MISSISSIPPI	6%	8%	None	Forfeit all interest, otherwise forfeit all interest and principal
MISSOURI	6%	10%	Unlimited	Liable for excess interest and invalidation of security agreement
MONTANA	6%	10%	Unlimited	Double the interest charged
NEBRASKA	6%	9%	Unlimited	Forfeit all interest
NEVADA	7%	12%	No statutory provision	Forfeit all interest
NEW HAMPSHIRE	6%	Unlimited	No limit	None
NEW JERSEY	7½%	None	No usury defense	Forfeit all interest
NEW MEXICO	6%	10%; 12% if no collateral	No usury defense	Forfeit all interest; recover 2X interest within two years of transaction (Charging usurious interest is a misdemeanor.)
NEW YORK	8%	8%	No rate	Contract void (Charging interest in excess of 25% per annum is a crime.)
NORTH CAROLINA	6%	8%	None	Forfeit all interest

STATE	LEGAL RATE	CONTRACT RATE	CORPORATE RATE	PENALTY
NORTH DAKOTA	4%	9%	Unlimited	Forfeit all interest and 25% of principal or double interest (Charging usurious interest is a misdemeanor.)
OHIO	6%	8%	No usury defense	Excess deducted from principal
OKLAHOMA	6%	10%	No usury defense	Repay excess or 10X excess if refund not made in reasonable time
OREGON	6%	10%	12%, no usury defense	Forfeit loan, less interest and payments of principal to school fund
PENNSYLVANIA	6% to $50,000	6%	No usury defense	Forfeit excess over legal interest
RHODE ISLAND	6%	21%	21%	Forfeit all interest and principal and contract void (Charging usurious interest is a misdemeanor.)
SOUTH CAROLINA	6%	8%	No usury defense	All interest plus costs (Charging usurious interest is a misdemeanor.)
SOUTH DAKOTA	6%	10%	No usury defense	Forfeit all interest (Charging illegal interest is a misdemeanor.)
TENNESSEE	6%	10%	No limit	Forfeit excess paid over 6% within two years
TEXAS	6%	10%	1½% per month, over $5,000 No usury defense	Forfeit double interest paid or all interest if rate is double rate allowed. Habitual violators of the usury may be enjoined by the courts

STATE	LEGAL RATE	CONTRACT RATE	CORPORATE RATE	PENALTY
UTAH	6%	As per U.C.C.	No special rate	10X excess if refund refused within a reasonable time (Charging usurious interest is a misdemeanor.)
VERMONT	7½%	12%	12%	Forfeit all interest and 50% of principal (Charging usurious interest is a misdemeanor.)
VIRGINIA	6%	8% No limit on partnerships professional associates real estate investments, etc.	None	Forfeit all interest
WASHINGTON	6%	12%	No statutory provision	Forfeit all interest
WEST VIRGINIA	6%	6%	No usury defense	Forfeit excess over 6%
WISCONSIN	5%	6%	Unlimited	Forfeit all interest plus principal under $2,000 (Charging usurious interest is a misdemeanor.)
WYOMING	7%	As determined by U.C.C.	No statutory rate	Greater amount between excess interest charged or 10X excess of refund refused within reasonable time after demand for refund is made

Exhibit 2
State and Local Consumer Protection Agencies

State Agencies

Alaska

Attorney General of Alaska
Pouch "K," State Capitol
Juneau, Alaska 99801

Arizona

Consumer Fraud Division
Office of the Attorney General
159 State Capitol Building
Phoenix, Arizona 85007

Arkansas

Consumer Protection Division
Office of Attorney General
Justice Building
Little Rock, Arkansas 72201

California

Consumer Fraud Section
Office of Attorney General
600 State Building
Los Angeles, California 90012

Director
Department of Consumer Affairs
1020 N. Street
Sacramento, California 95814

Colorado

Office of Consumer Affairs
Attorney General of Colorado
503 Farmers Union Building
1575 Sherman Street
Denver, Colorado 80203

Connecticut

Commissioner, Department of Consumer Protection
State Office Building
Hartford, Connecticut 06115

Delaware

Consumer Protection Division
Office of Attorney General
1206 King Street
Wilmington, Delaware 19801

Florida

Attorney General of Florida
State Capitol
Tallahassee, Florida 32304

Division of Consumer Affairs
Florida Department of Agricultural
and Consumer Services
The Capitol
Tallahassee, Florida 32304

Georgia

Georgia Consumer Services Program
Department of Family and Child
Services
15 Peachtree Street, Room 909
Atlanta, Georgia 30303

Hawaii

Director of Consumer Protection
Office of the Governor
602 Kamamalu Building
250 South King Street
P. O. Box 3767
Honolulu, Hawaii 96811

Idaho

Consumer Protection Division
Office of Attorney General
State Capitol
Boise, Idaho 83707

Illinois

Consumer Fraud Section
Office of Attorney General
134 N. LaSalle Street
Chicago, Illinois   60602

Indiana

Attorney General of Indiana
219 State House
Indianapolis, Indiana   46204

Consumer Advisory Council
c/o Indiana Department of Commerce
336 State House
Indianapolis, Indiana   46204

Iowa

Consumer Fraud Division
Office of Attorney General
1223 E. Court Street
Des Moines, Iowa   50319

Kansas

Consumer Protection Division
Office of Attorney General
The Capitol
Topeka, Kansas   66612

Kentucky

Consumer Protection Division
Office of Attorney General
The Capitol
Frankfort, Kentucky 40601

Executive Director
Citizen's Commission for Consumer Protection
State Capitol
Frankfort, Kentucky   40601

Maine

Consumer Protection Division
Office of Attorney General
State House
Augusta, Maine   04330

Maryland

Consumer Protection Division
Office of Attorney General
1200 One Charles Center
Baltimore, Maryland   21201

Massachusetts

Consumer Protection Division
Office of Attorney General
State House
Boston, Massachusetts   02133

Executive Secretary
Massachusetts Consumers' Council
State Office Building, Government Center
100 Cambridge Street
Boston, Massachusetts   02202

Michigan

Consumer Protection Division
Office of Attorney General
Law Building
Lansing, Michigan   48902

Assistant to the Governor for Consumer Affairs
1033 South Washington Street
Lansing, Michigan   48910

Executive Director
Michigan Consumer Council
525 Hollister Building
108 W. Allegan
Lansing, Michigan   48933

Minnesota

Special Assistant Attorney General
for Consumer Protection
Attorney General of Minnesota
102 State Capitol
St. Paul, Minnesota   55101

Office of Consumer Services
Department of Commerce, Room 230
State Office Building
St. Paul, Minnesota   55101

Mississippi

Assistant Attorney General for Consumer Protection
Attorney General of Mississippi
State Capitol
Jackson, Mississippi 39001

Consumer Protection Division
Department of Agriculture and Commerce
Jackson, Mississippi 39205

Missouri

Consumer Protection Division
Office of Attorney General
Supreme Court Building
Jefferson City, Missouri 65101

New Hampshire

Assistant Attorney General for Consumer Protection
Office of Attorney General
State House Annex
Concord, New Hampshire 03301

New Jersey

Office of Consumer Protection
1100 Raymond Boulevard
Newark, New Jersey 07102

New Mexico

Consumer Protection Division
Office of Attorney General
Supreme Court Building Box 2246
Santa Fe, New Mexico 87501

New York

Consumer Frauds and Protection Bureau
Office of the Attorney General
80 Centre Street
New York, New York 10013

Chairman and Executive Director
Consumer Protection Board
380 Madison Avenue
New York, New York 10017

North Carolina

Consumer Protection and Anti-Trust Division
Office of Attorney General
P. O. Box 629
Raleigh, North Carolina 27602

North Dakota

Consumer Protection Division
Office of Attorney General
The Capitol
Bismarck, North Dakota 58501

Ohio

Consumer Frauds and Crimes Section
Office of Attorney General
State House Annex
Columbus, Ohio 43215

Oklahoma

Administrator
Department of Consumer Affairs
Lincoln Office Plaza, Suite 74
4545 Lincoln Boulevard
Oklahoma City, Oklahoma 73105

Oregon

Assistant Attorney General for Antitrust and Consumer Protection
Office of Attorney General
322 State Office Building
Salem, Oregon 97310

Assistant to the Governor for Economic Development and Consumer Services
State Capitol Building
Salem, Oregon 97310

Pennsylvania

Bureau of Consumer Protection
Pennsylvania Department of Justice
2–4 N. Market Square (Durbin Building)
Harrisburg, Pennsylvania 17101

Rhode Island

Special Assistant Attorney General
for Consumer Protection
Office of Attorney General
Providence, Rhode Island 02903

Executive Director
Rhode Island Consumers' Council
Providence, Rhode Island 02902

South Dakota

Office of Consumer Affairs
Attorney General of South Dakota
State Capitol
Pierre, South Dakota 57501

Texas

Antitrust and Consumer Protection
Division
Office of Attorney General
Capitol Station, P.O. Box 12548
Austin, Texas 78711

Office of Consumer Credit
1011 San Jacinto Boulevard
P. O. Box 2107
Austin, Texas 78767

Utah

Assistant Attorney General for Consumer Protection
Office of Attorney General
State Capitol
Salt Lake City, Utah 84114

Administration of Consumer
Credit
103 State Capitol
Salt Lake City, Utah 84114

Vermont

Consumer Protection Bureau
Office of Attorney General
#4 Church Street
Burlington, Vermont 05401

Family Economics and Home Management Specialist
Room 210, Terrill Hall
University of Vermont
Burlington, Vermont 05401

Virginia

Assistant Attorney General for Consumer Protection
Office of the Attorney General
Supreme Court—Library Building
Richmond, Virginia 23219

Special Assistant to the Governor
on Minority Groups and Consumer
Affairs
Office of the Governor
Richmond, Virginia 23219

Administrator of Consumer Affairs
Department of Agriculture and
Commerce
8th Street Office Building
Richmond, Virginia 23219

Washington

Consumer Protection and Anti-trust
Division
Office of the Attorney General
1266 Dexter Horton Building
Seattle, Washington 98104

West Virginia

Assistant Attorney General for Consumer Affairs
Office of Attorney General
The Capitol
Charleston, West Virginia 25305

Consumer Protection Division
West Virginia Department of Labor
1900 Washington Street East
Charleston, West Virginia 25305

Wisconsin

Assistant Attorney General for Consumer Protection
Office of Attorney General
Department of Justice
Madison, Wisconsin 53702

Bureau of Consumer Protection
Trade Division
Department of Agriculture
801 West Badger Road
Madison, Wisconsin 53713

Wyoming

State Examiner and Administrator
Consumer Credit Code
State Supreme Court Building
Cheyenne, Wyoming 82001

*Commonwealth of Puerto Rico
and the Virgin Islands*

Attorney General of Puerto Rico
P. O. Box 192
San Juan, Puerto Rico 00902

Consumer Services Administration
P. O. Box 13934
Santurce, Puerto Rico 00908

Executive Director
Public Services Dom.
Charlotte Amalie, St. Thomas Virgin Islands 00801

Local Agencies

Los Angeles, California

Secretary
Los Angeles Consumer Protection Committee
107 South Broadway
Los Angeles, California 90012

San Francisco, California

Secretary, Bay Area Consumer Protection Coordinating Committee
450 Golden Gate Avenue
Box 36005
San Francisco, California 94102

Santa Clara County, California

Director
Santa Clara County Department of Weights and Measures and Consumer Affairs
Division of Consumer Affairs
409 Matthew Street
Santa Clara, California 95050

Dade County, Florida

Director
Consumer Protection Division
1351 N.W. 12th Street
Miami, Florida 33125

Jacksonville, Florida

Consumer Affairs Officer
Division of Consumer Affairs
264 First Avenue North
St. Petersburg, Florida 33701

Chicago, Illinois

Commissioner, Department of Consumer Sales and Weights and Measures
City Hall
121 North LaSalle Street
Chicago, Illinois 60602

121

Secretary
Chicago Consumer Protection
Committee
Room 486 U.S. Court House and
Federal Office Building
219 South Dearborn Street
Chicago, Illinois   60604

Louisville, Kentucky

Division of Weights and Measures
and Consumer Affairs
Metropolitan Sewer District Building, Second Floor
Louisville, Kentucky   40202

New Orleans, Louisiana

Secretary
Consumer Protection Committee
of New Orleans
1000 Masonic Temple Building
333 St. Charles Street
New Orleans, Louisiana   70130

Prince Georges County, Maryland

Consumer Protection Division
Prince Georges County Court-
house
Upper Marlboro, Maryland   20870

Boston, Massachusetts

Chairman, Boston Consumer's Coun-
cil
Office of the Mayor
Boston City Hall
Boston, Massachusetts   02201

Secretary
Boston Metropolitan Consumer
Protection Committee
c/o Federal Trade Commission
John Fitzgerald Kennedy Federal
Building, Government Center
Boston, Massachusetts   02203

Detroit, Michigan

Secretary, Detroit Consumer Protec-
tion Coordinating Committee
Immigration and Naturalization
Building
33 Mt. Elliot Avenue
Detroit, Michigan   48207

St. Louis, Missouri

Chairman, Citizens Consumer Advisory Committee
7701 Forsyth Boulevard
Clayton, Missouri   63105

Camden County, New Jersey

Director, Camden County Office of
Consumer Affairs Room 606
Commerce Building
#1 Broadway
Camden, New Jersey   08101

Long Beach (Long Island), New York

Director, Consumers Affairs
City Hall
Long Beach, New York   11561

Nassau County, New York

Commissioner, Office of Consumer
Affairs
160 Old Country Road
Mineola, New York   11501

New York City, New York

Commissioner, City of New York Department of Consumer Affairs
80 Lafayette Street
New York, New York   10013

Columbus, Ohio

City Sealer of Weights and Measures
City Hall
Columbus, Ohio   43215

122

Multnomah County, Oregon

Deputy District Attorney in Charge
of Consumer Protection
600 County Court House
Portland, Oregon 97204

Philadelphia, Pennsylvania

Secretary, Philadelphia Consumer
Protection Committee
53 Long Lane
Upper Darby, Pennsylvania 19082

Consumer Protection Office
City Hall Room 121
Philadelphia, Pennsylvania 19107

Exhibit 3 Garnishee Requirements of each State

In each state the following property is exempt from garnishment:

ARIZONA 50% of earnings for thirty days prior to levy for use of family.

ALABAMA 30% of weekly disposable income or amount by which disposable earnings per week are in excess of 50 times federal minimum hourly wage.

ALASKA Earnings of judgment debtor not to exceed $350 for head of family, $200 for single man for personal services rendered within 30 days preceding levy of execution where necessary to support debtor's family.

ARKANSAS Wages for sixty days exempt provided statement is filed that wages are less than $200 if single, and $500 for a family. First $25 a week net wages exempt.

CALIFORNIA Greater of 50% or portion exempt by federal statute of the earnings of the defendant or judgment debtor received for his personal services rendered at any time within thirty days next preceding the levy of attachment or execution.

COLORADO Earnings 70%, 35% if single.

CONNECTICUT Greater amount 75% of disposable earnings per week up to greater of $65 or amount equal to 40 times federal minimum hourly wage.

DELAWARE Earnings: 90% in New Castle County, 60% in Kent and Sussex, not exempt if self-employed. Liability for balance applies only to necessities of life.

DISTRICT OF COLUMBIA Greater of 75% of disposable earnings per week or amount of disposable earnings per week equal to 30 times federal minimum hourly wage. Withhold by garnishee-employer 90% of first $200 of gross wages, payable in a month in excess of $200 and under $500.

FLORIDA All earnings exempt except for alimony and support payments at discretion of court.

GEORGIA Greater of 75% of disposable earnings per week or amount by which disposable earnings exceed 30 times the federal minimum hourly wage.

HAWAII 95% of first $100, 90% of next $100, and 80% of gross wages in excess of $200 per month or equivalent per week.

IDAHO	Earnings 75% for his personal service rendered within thirty days preceding levy if necessary for use of family supported by his labor; provided that if garnishment be founded upon debt for necessaries, exemption shall not exceed 50% of wages or salary due at time of service of execution or attachment. In no case shall exemption exceed $100 at any one time.
ILLINOIS	Earnings: 85% with minimum of $50 per week if single, or $65 if head of household, and maximum of $200 per week.
INDIANA	75% of disposable earnings per week in excess of 30 times federal minimum hourly wage.
IOWA	75% of disposable earnings for week or amount by which disposable earnings exceed 30 times federal minimum hourly wage, whichever is greater. Maximum amount that can be garnished in any year is $250 for each creditor.
KANSAS	75% of disposable earnings for week or amount by which disposable earnings exceed 30 times federal minimum hourly wage, whichever is greater. Exemption inapplicable to support orders.
KENTUCKY	Greater of 75% of disposable income per week or amount by which disposable earnings exceed 30 times federal minimum hourly wage. Exemption inapplicable to support orders.
LOUISIANA	75% of disposable earnings for any week, but not less than $70 on loans in excess of 10%. Lenders forbidden to use garnishment.
MAINE	Greater of 75% of disposable earnings for week or any amount by which disposable earnings exceed 10 times federal minimum hourly wage.
MARYLAND	Wages $150 exempt multiplied by the number of weeks in which said wages were earned or 75% of such wages, whichever is greater; except that in Caroline, Worcester, Kent and Queen Anne counties, exemption for any work week shall be greater of 75% of wages due or 30 times federal minimum hourly wage.
MASSACHU-SETTS	Wages for personal labor or services exempted from attachment to amount of $125 per week. Exemption of $75 of personal income which is not otherwise exempt by law.
MICHIGAN	Householder with family, 60% exemption with following limitations: On first garnishment, maximum $50 per week for labor of one week. For more than one week's labor, maximum $90 and minimum $60. As to subsequent garnishments for one week's

labor, maximum per week is $60 and minimum $24. For a period of more than 16 days, maximum is $60 and minimum $30. Employee, not householder with family, first garnishment 40% exemption with $50 maximum, $20 maximum and $10 minimum.

MINNESOTA   75% of net wages due at time of attachment, garnishment, or levy or 8 times the number of business days and paid holidays, not greater than 5 per week in the pay period, times the federal minimum hourly wage, whichever is greater. Where debtor has been on relief, exemption for a period of six months from date of return to private employment.

MISSISSIPPI   75% of wages or salaries of resident laborer or employee.

MISSOURI   Greater of (1) 75% of weekly earnings (2) weekly amount equal to 30 times federal minimum hourly wage or (3) 90% of work week earnings.

MONTANA   All earnings for forty-five days preceding garnishment, limited to 50% exemption.

NEBRASKA   Greatest of 75% of disposable earnings or amount equal to 30 times federal minimum hourly wage or 85% of disposable earnings if wage earner is head of family.

NEVADA   The greater of 75% of disposable earnings or the amount by which disposable earnings exceed 30 times the minimum federal hourly wage.

NEW HAMPSHIRE   Wages for labor performed after service of writ: wages for labor performed before service exempt unless action founded on debt on judgment issued by state court. In such cases wages equal to 50 times federal minimum hourly wage are exempt. Special exemption for small loan law debts.

NEW JERSEY   Earnings 90% if debtor earns $7,500 a year or less minimum. If more than $7,500, garnishee fixed by court.

NEW MEXICO   Greater of 75% of debtor's disposable earnings or of excess of 40 times federal minimum hourly wage rate. Disposable earnings is that part of the debtor's salary remaining after deduction of amounts required to be withheld by law.

NEW YORK   Earnings 90%, unless less than $85 per week is earned. Balance is payable as installments.

NORTH CAROLINA   Earnings sixty days, preceding garnishee, if necessary for support of family.

NORTH DAKOTA	Greater of 75% of debtor's disposable earnings or of excess of 40 times federal minimum hourly wage.
OHIO	Greater of 82½% of the debtor's disposable income or 175 times federal minimum hourly wage. Statutory scheme preempted by Federal Consumer Protection Act.
OKLAHOMA	Earnings: 75% ninety days: 100% shown to be necessaries for support of family; single man, 75% of wages.
OREGON	Greater of 75% of disposable earnings for week or amounts by which disposable earnings exceed 30 times the federal minimum hourly wage.
PENNSYLVANIA	100% of all wages. Does not apply to support orders of court.
RHODE ISLAND	Earnings: $50 plus salary and wages of dependents; 100% for seamen; 100% for debtor on relief; and all earnings one year after off relief.
SOUTH DAKOTA	100% of all earnings within sixty days, if necessary for support of family. However, 15% may be attached for judgment for food, fuel, or medicines.
TENNESSEE	Wages to 50%, minimum $20, maximum $50 per week, if single 40%, $17.50 and $40 per week respectively; $2.50 per week addition for each dependent.
TEXAS	All wages for personal services.
UTAH	Married man or head of family: one half of earnings for 30 days prior to levy if his earnings are necessary for family support. Minimum exemption of $50 per month on judgments arising from debts on consumer credit sales greater of 75% disposable earnings per week or 30 times federal minimum hourly wage.
VERMONT	75% of disposable earnings for week or excess of 30 times federal minimum hourly wage, whichever is greater.
VIRGINIA	75% of disposable earnings for that week or excess of 30 times federal minimum hourly wage, whichever is greater. Exemption is inapplicable to court order for support.
WASHINGTON	The greater part of 40 times of the state hourly minimum wage or of 75% of disposable earnings of defendant is exempt from garnishment. Disposable earnings means that part of the earnings remaining after deductions of the amount required by law to be withheld.

WEST VIRGINIA	$20 per week minimum of 80% of wages due or to become due within one year after issuance of execution.
WISCONSIN	Greater of 75% of debtor's disposable earnings or excess of 30 times federal minimum hourly wage rate. Disposable earnings means that part of earnings after deduction of amount required by law to be withheld. Employees with dependents: basic exemptions, $120 plus $20 per dependent for each 30-day period prior to service of process. Maximum exemption, 75% of income. Employees without dependents, basic exemption of 60% of income for each 30-day period prior to service of process. Minimum $75. Maximum $100.
WYOMING	Judgments on consumer credit sales, home or loan, greater of 75% of disposable earnings or excess over 30 times federal minimum hourly wage. Otherwise 50% of earnings for personal service 60 days before levy if necessary for use of resident family.

Form 1 Notice to Consumer of Right to Rescind Certain Contracts

S 148– Notice of Right to Rescind: Truth in Lending Act :
Federal Reserve Regulation Z: 7-1-69
[illegible]

COPYRIGHT 1969 BY JULIUS BLUMBERG. INC., LAW BLANK PUBLISHERS
80 EXCHANGE PLACE AT BROADWAY, NEW YORK

NOTICE TO CUSTOMER REQUIRED BY FEDERAL LAW:

IDENTIFICATION OF TRANSACTION:

....

....

TO CUSTOMER:

⌐   ¬

....

....

└   ┘

You have entered into a transaction on   19   which may result in a lien, mortgage, or other security interest on your home. You have a legal right under Federal Law to cancel this transaction, if you desire to do so, without any penalty or obligation within three business days from the above date or any later date on which all material disclosures required under the Truth in Lending Act have been given to you. If you so cancel the transaction, any lien, mortgage, or other security interest on your home arising from this transaction is automatically void. You are also entitled to receive a refund of any down payment or other consideration if you cancel. If you decide to cancel this transaction, you

may do so by notifying ....

....

by mail or telegram sent not later than midnight of   19   . **You may also use any other form of written notice identifying the transaction if it is delivered to the above address not later than that time. This notice may be used for that purpose by dating and signing below.**

I hereby cancel this transaction.

....**19**........   ....
          Date   Customer's Signature

EFFECT OF RESCISSION. When a customer exercises his right to rescind under paragraph (a) of this section, he is not liable for any finance or other charge, and any security interest becomes void upon such a rescission. Within 10 days after receipt of a notice of rescission, the creditor shall return to the customer any money or property given as earnest money, downpayment, or otherwise, and shall take any action necessary or appropriate to reflect the termination of any security interest created under the transaction. If the creditor has delivered any property to the customer, the customer may retain possession of it. Upon the performance of the creditor's obligations under this section, the customer shall tender the property to the creditor, except that if return of the property in kind would be impracticable or inequitable, the customer shall tender its reasonable value. Tender shall be made at the location of the property or at the residence of the customer, at the option of the customer. If the creditor does not take possession of the property within 10 days after tender by the customer, ownership of the property vests in the customer without obligation on his part to pay for it.

Form 2 Sample Property Execution

B 320—Execution Against Property, To Sheriff, Marshal, Notice to Garnishee, Enforcement of Money Judgment. Civil Court. 9-63
6 blanks suggested: original; office copy; 2 copies each for debtor and garnishee if officer cannot serve personally.

COPYRIGHT 1963 BY JULIUS BLUMBERG, INC., LAW BLANK PUBLISHERS
80 EXCHANGE PLACE AT BROADWAY, NEW YORK

CIVIL COURT OF THE CITY OF NEW YORK,
COUNTY OF   QUEENS

Index No.

33012/73

WATING AND WATING

                     Plaintiff

against

RICHARD SIX

                     Defendant

*EXECUTION
WITH NOTICE TO
GARNISHEE*

The People of the State of New York

TO THE SHERIFF OR ANY MARSHAL OF THE CITY OF NEW YORK, GREETING:

WHEREAS, *in an action in the Civil Court of the City of New York, County of*   QUEENS
between   WATING AND WATING

                                       as plaintiff   *and*

RICHARD SIX

                                       as defendant

who are all the parties named in said action, a judgment was entered on   April 18,   *19* 73
in favor of   WATING AND WATING   *judgment creditor*
and against   RICHARD SIX   *judgment debtor*
whose last known address is   250-33 Union Turnpike, Bellerose, New York
in the amount of $ 3300.00   *including costs, of which $* 3300.00   *together*
with interest thereon from   April 18, 1973   *remains due and unpaid;*

NOW, THEREFORE, WE COMMAND YOU *to satisfy the said judgment out of the personal property of the above named judgment debtor and the debts due to him; and that only the property in which said judgment debtor who is not deceased has an interest or the debts owed to him shall be levied upon or sold hereunder; AND TO RETURN this execution to the clerk of the above captioned court within sixty days after issuance unless service of this execution is made within that time or within extensions of that time made in writing by the attorney(s) for the judgment creditor*

Notice to Garnishee

TO: First National City Bank
ADDRESS: 300 Union Turnpike, Bellerose, New York

WHEREAS, *it appears that you are indebted to the judgment debtor, above named, or in possession or custody of property not capable of delivery in which the judgment debtor has an interest, including, without limitation, the following specified debt and property:* All monies deposited by judgment debtor and balance in passbook 390112, in the name of the judgment debtor.

NOW, THEREFORE, YOU ARE REQUIRED *by section 5232(a) of the Civil Practice Law and Rules forthwith to transfer to the said sheriff or marshal all personal property not capable of delivery in which the judgment debtor is known or believed to have an interest now in or hereafter coming into your possession or custody including any property specified in this notice; and to pay to the said sheriff or marshal, upon maturity, all debts now due or hereafter coming due from you to the judgment debtor, including any debts specified in this notice; and to execute any documents necessary to effect such transfer or payment;*

AND TAKE NOTICE *that until such transfer or payment is made or until the expiration of ninety days after the service of this execution upon you or such further time as is provided by any order of the court served upon you whichever event first occurs, you are forbidden to make or suffer any sale, assignment or transfer of, or any interference with, any such property, or pay over or otherwise dispose of any such debt, to any person other than said sheriff or marshal, except upon direction of said sheriff or marshal or pursuant to an order of the court;*

AND TAKE FURTHER NOTICE THAT *at the expiration of ninety days after a levy is made by service of this execution, or of such further time as the court upon motion of the judgment creditor has provided, this levy shall be void except as to property or debts which have been transferred or paid to said sheriff or marshal or as to which a proceeding under sections 5225 or 5227 of the Civil Practice Law and Rules has been brought.*

WITNESS, Honorable   JOE JUDGE   , *one of the judges of our said*
Civil Court at the City of New York, dated the   30   *day of*   September   *19* 73.

Joe Sharpe

The name signed must be printed beneath.

JOE SHARPE

*Attorney(s) for Judgment Creditor
Office and Post Office Address*

111-20   Jamaica Avenue
Jamaica, New York   11432

Form 3   Sample Homestead Exemption

___

JOHN DOE and MARY DOE, his wife, both residing at 11–12 110th Street, Jamaica, New York, hereby claim an exemption of $2,000. pursuant to Section 5206 of the CPLR as said premises in which they live, more fully described below, are occupied as a principal residence by said JOHN DOE and his wife, MARY DOE, and is, therefore, exempt from application to the satisfaction of a money judgment for the aforesaid amount.

Description of the property claimed exempt and to be the premises at 11–12 110th Street, Jamaica, New York, is described as follows:

"ALL that certain parcel of land with the buildings and improvements thereon erected in the Borough of Queens, County of Queens, City and State of New York, bounded and described as follows:

BEGINNING at the corner formed by the intersection of the northerly side of 11th Avenue with the easterly side of 110th Street running thence northerly along the easterly side of 110th Street; 100 feet; thence easterly parallel with the northerly side of 11th Avenue, 40 feet; thence southerly parallel with the easterly side of 110th Street, 100 feet to the northerly side of 11th Avenue; thence westerly along the northerly side of 11th Avenue, 40 feet to the corner aforesaid at the BEGINNING"

SUBJECT TO: State of facts shown on Survey made by Richard Smith dated October 31, 1963.

```
_____
JOHN DOE

_____
MARY DOE
```

STATE OF NEW YORK)
COUNTY OF QUEENS) SS:

On the 10th day of January, 1973 before me personally came JOHN DOE and MARY DOE, to me known to be the individuals described in and who executed the foregoing instrument, and acknowledged that they executed the same.

(Notary)

Form 4 Sample of "Straight" Bankruptcy Petition

In the District Court of the United States for the   Eastern   District of   New York

In the matter of

JOHN SMITH,

> In Bankruptcy
>
> No....................

See footnote   Bankrupt

PETITION

To the Honorable Judges of the District Court of the United States

for the   Eastern   District of   New York :

THE PETITION of   JOHN SMITH
residing at   100 Center Street, Mineola, L.I.,
County of   Nassau   State of   New York
by occupation a   truck driver
and employed by   A B C Oil Company, New York City, New York

XXXXXXXXXXXXXXXXXXXXXXX

who states that   he has not conducted any business or used any assumed, trade or any other names or designations during the past six years, other than as set forth in the above caption,

RESPECTFULLY REPRESENTS:

1. Your petitioner has had his principal place of business [or has resided, or has had his domicile] XX has resided at 100 Center Street, Mineola, and had a business address at 250 Summit Street, New York City, N.Y., within the above judicial district, for a longer portion of the six months immediately preceding the filing of this petition than in any other judicial district.

2. Your petitioner owes debts and is willing to surrender all his property for the benefit of his creditors, except such as is exempt by law, and desires to obtain the benefit of the Act of Congress relating to bankruptcy.

3. The schedule hereto annexed, marked Schedule A, and verified by your petitioner's oath, contains a full and true statement of all his debts, and, so far as it is possible to ascertain, the names and places of residence of his creditors, and such further statements concerning said debts as are required by the provisions of said Act.

4. The schedule hereto annexed, marked Schedule B, and verified by your petitioner's oath, contains an accurate inventory of all his property, real and personal, and such further statements concerning said property as are required by the provisions of said Act.

WHEREFORE your petitioner prays that he may be adjudged by the court to be a bankrupt within the purview of said Act.

....
JOHN SMITH   *Petitioner*

....
JOE ATTORNEY   *Attorney*

STATE OF   NEW YORK
                    } ss.:
COUNTY OF   NASSAU

I,   JOHN SMITH   , the petitioner named in the foregoing petition, do hereby make solemn oath that the statements contained therein are true according to the best of my knowledge, information, and belief.

Subscribed and sworn to before me this
1st   day of   November   19 73

....
JOHN SMITH   *Petitioner*

....
NOTARY PUBLIC : STATE OF NEW YORK

             (*Official Character*)

NOTE: Set forth in caption all assumed, trade and any other names or designations by or under which bankrupt or debtor has been known or has conducted any business within preceding 6 years.

Form 4 *(continued)*

Official Form No. 2

JULIUS BLUMBERG, INC., LAW BLANK PUBLISHERS
80 EXCHANGE PLACE, AT BROADWAY, NEW YORK

STATEMENT OF AFFAIRS
(For Bankrupt or Debtor Not Engaged in Business.)

(NOTE:—Each question should be answered or the failure to answer explained. If the answer is "none," this should be stated. If additional space is needed for the answer to any question, a separate sheet, properly identified and made a part hereof, should be used and attached. The term, "original petition," as used in the following questions, shall mean the petition filed under section 3b or 4a of chapter III, section 322 of chapter XI, section 422 of chapter XII, or section 622 of chapter XIII.)

1. Name and residence.
   a. What is your full name?   JOHN SMITH

   b. Where do you now reside?   100 Center Street, Mineola, L.I., New York.

   c. Where else have you resided during the six years immediately preceding the filing of the original petition herein?

   111 Belmont Avenue, Islip, New York.

2. Occupation and income.
   a. What is your occupation?   Truck driver

   b. Where are you now employed?
   (Give the name and address of your employer, or the address at which you carry on your trade or profession, and the length of time you have been so employed.)
   A B C Oil Company, New York City, New York.

   c. Have you been in partnership with anyone, or engaged in any business, during the six years immediately preceding the filing of the original petition herein? (If so, give particulars, including names, dates and places.) No partnerships. Have been in business for myself as X Y Z Floor Waxing Service from Jan. 19, 1966 to April 1971. XYZ Floor Waxing Service was located at 100 Center Street, Mineola, L.I., N.Y.; and Mineola Stationery, 111 Second St., Mineola, L.I., N.Y. from September, 1971 to December 1972.

   d. What amount of income have you received from your trade or profession during each of the two years immediately preceding the filing of the original petition herein?

   1971: $1025.37 wages; $76.54 business income; $717.66 sales of property; Total 1961:
   1972: $4,044.70 from self-employment $1,819.59
   e. What amount of income have you received from other sources during each of these two years?
   (Give particulars, including each source, and the amount received therefrom.)

   None

3. Income tax returns.
   a. Where did you file your last federal and state income tax returns, and for what years?

   Federal: filed in Brooklyn   1972
   New York State: Filed in Brooklyn 1972

4. Bank accounts and safe deposit boxes.
   a. What bank accounts have you maintained, alone or together with any other person, and in your own or any other name, within the two years immediately preceding the filing of the original petition herein? (Give the name and address of each bank, the name in which the deposit was maintained, and the name of every person authorized to make withdrawals from such account.)

   1. National City Bank, Jamaica, New York (special checking account in names of John Smith and Joan Smith)
   2. Valley National Bank, Floral Park, N.Y., in names of John Smith and Joan Smith.
   3. Hempstead Bank, Mineola, N.Y. (business checking acct. in name of John Smith).

   b. What safe deposit box or boxes or other depository or depositories have you kept or used for your securities, cash or other valuables, within the two years immediately preceding the filing of the original petition herein?
   (Give the name and address of the bank or other depository, the name in which each box or other depository was kept, the name of every person who had the right of access thereto, a brief description of the contents thereof, and, if surrendered, when surrendered; or, if transferred, when transferred and the name and address of the transferee.)

   None

5. Books and records.
   a. Have you kept books of account or records relating to your affairs within the two years immediately preceding the filing of the original petition herein?   Yes

   b. In whose possession are these books or records?
   (Give names and addresses.)   John Smith, 100 Center Street, Mineola, L.I., New York.

   c. Have you destroyed any books of account or records relating to your affairs within the two years immediately preceding the filing of the original petition herein? (If so, give particulars, including date of destruction and reason therefor.)

   No.

6. Property held in trust.
   a. What property do you hold in trust for any other person?
   (Give name and address of each person, and a description of the property and the amount or value thereof.)

   None.

Form 4 *(continued)*

Official Form No. 2 Continued

JULIUS BLUMBERG, INC., LAW BLANK PUBLISHERS
80 EXCHANGE PLACE, AT BROADWAY, NEW YORK

STATEMENT OF AFFAIRS—Continued

7. Prior bankruptcy or other proceedings; assignments for benefit of creditors.

a. What proceedings under the Bankruptcy Act have been brought by or against you during the six years immediately preceding the filing of the original petition herein? (Give the location of the bankruptcy court, the nature of the proceeding, and whether a discharge was granted or refused, or a composition, arrangement or plan was or was not confirmed.)

> None

b. Was any of your property, at the time of the filing of the original petition herein, in the hands of a receiver or trustee? (If so, give the name and location of the court, nature of the proceeding, a brief description of the property, and name of receiver or trustee.)

> No.

c. Have you made any assignment of your property for the benefit of your creditors, or any general settlement with your creditors, within the two years immediately preceding the filing of the original petition herein? (If so, give dates, the name of the assignee, and a brief statement of the terms of assignment or settlement.)

> No.

8. Suits, executions and attachments.

a. Have you been party plaintiff or defendant in any suit within the year immediately preceding the filing of the original petition herein? (If so, give the name and location of the court, the title and nature of the proceeding, and the result.) I was a defendant
in an action in the Second District Court of the County of Nassau, index 444/73, at Hempstead, in an action brought by Fred Allen, as landlord, for monies due. Judgment was entered against me for $937.16 on June 28, 1973. A transcript thereof was filed in the Nassau County Clerk's Office on July 11, 1973.

b. Has any execution or attachment been levied against your property within the four months immediately preceding the filing of the original petition herein? (If so, give particulars, including property seized and at whose suit.)
> No.

9. Loans repaid.

a. What repayments of loans have you made during the year immediately preceding the filing of the original petition herein? (Give the name and address of the lender, the amount of the loan and when received, the amount and date when repaid, and, if the lender is a relative, the relationship.)

1. First National City Bank loan for $1600. in April, 1971; repaid Nov. 31, 1972,
2. General Loan Corp., Mineola, N.Y. $1800. approx. financed in 1960. In Jan. 1973, I repaid loan by making monthly payments and b · selling 1970 Chevrolet for $750.00, which was given to General Loan Corp.

10. Transfer of property.

a. What property have you transferred or otherwise disposed of during the year immediately preceding the filing of the original petition herein? (Give a description of the property, the date of the transfer or disposition, to whom transferred or how disposed of, and, if the transferee is a relative, the relationship, the consideration, if any, received therefor, and the disposition of such consideration.)

House and lot at 100 Center Street, Mineola, New York, transferred to my mother, Anna Smith, in consideration of $3,500.00 loaned to me by her prior to the transfer.

11. Losses.

a. Have you suffered any losses from fire, theft or gambling during the year immediately preceding the filing of the original petition herein? (If so, give particulars, including dates, and the amounts of money or value and general description of property lost.)

> No.

State of NEW YORK

County of NASSAU   } ss.:

JOHN SMITH   *Bankrupt [or Debtor]*

I,   JOHN SMITH   , the person who subscribed to the foregoing statement of affairs, do hereby make solemn oath that the answers therein contained are true and complete to the best of my knowledge, information, and belief.

JOHN SMITH   *Bankrupt [or Debtor]*

Subscribed and sworn to before me this 1st day of November , 19 73

NOTARY PUBLIC : STATE OF NEW YORK
[Official character]

134

1001—Official Form.

JULIUS BLUMBERG, INC., LAW BLANK PUBLISHERS
80 EXCHANGE PLACE, AT BROADWAY, NEW YORK

SCHEDULE A.—STATEMENT OF ALL DEBTS OF DEBTOR
Schedule A-1
Statement of all creditors to whom priority is secured by the act.

Claims which have priority.	Reference to ledger or voucher.	Names of creditors.	Residences (if unknown, that fact must be stated.)	When and where incurred or contracted.	Whether claim is contingent, unliquidated or disputed.	Nature and consideration of the debt, and whether incurred or contracted as partner or joint contractor and, if so, with whom.	Amount due or claimed.	
a. Wages due workmen, servants, clerks, or traveling or city salesmen on salary or commission basis, whole or part time, whether or not selling exclusively for the debtor, to an amount not exceeding $600 each, earned within three months before filing the petition.		None				$	00	00
b. Taxes due and owing to— (1) The United States.		None						
(2) The State of N.Y.		None						
(3) The county, district, or municipality of		None						
State of		None					00	00
c. (1) Debts owing to any person, including the United States, who by the laws of the United States is entitled to priority.		None						
(2) Rent owing to a landlord who is entitled to priority by the laws of the State of		None						
accrued within three months before filing the petition, for actual use and occupancy.							00	00
						Total		

JOHN SMITH
_____ **Petitioner**

Form 4 *(continued)*

JULIUS BLUMBERG, INC., LAW BLANK PUBLISHERS
80 EXCHANGE PLACE, AT BROADWAY, NEW YORK

SCHEDULE A.—STATEMENT OF ALL DEBTS OF DEBTOR (Continued)
Schedule A-2.
Creditors holding securities

(N. B.—Particulars of securities held, with dates of same, and when they were given, to be stated under the names of the several creditors, and also particulars concerning each debt, as required by the Act of Congress relating to bankruptcy, and whether contracted as partner or joint contractor with any other person ; and if so, with whom.)

Reference to ledger or voucher.	Names of creditors.	Residences (if unknown, that fact must be stated.)	Description of securities	When and where debts were contracted, and nature and consideration thereof.	Whether claim is contingent, unliquidated or disputed.	Value of securities.	Amount due or claimed.	
						$	$	
	None						00	00
							00	00
					Total_____		00	00

JOHN SMITH   𝔓etitioner

136

Form 4 *(continued)*

1003—Official Form.

JULIUS BLUMBERS, INC., LAW BLANK PUBLISHERS
80 EXCHANGE PLACE, AT BROADWAY, NEW YORK

SCHEDULE A-3.
Creditors whose claims are unsecured.

(N. B.—When the name and residence (or either) of any drawer, maker, indorser, or holder of any bill or note, etc., are unknown, the fact must be stated, and also the name and residence of the last holder known to the debtor. The debt due to each creditor must be stated in full, and any claim by way of set-off stated in the schedule of property.)

Reference to ledger or voucher.	Names of creditors.	Residences (If unknown, that fact must be stated.)	When and where contracted.	Whether claim is contingent, unliquidated or disputed.	Nature and consideration of the debt, and whether any judgment, bond, bill of exchange, promissory note, etc., and whether contracted as partner or joint contractor with any other person; and, if so, with whom.	Amount due or claimed.	
	Jones & Jones, Esqs., 100 Broadway, New York, N.Y.; contracted Jan. 1-July 11, 1973; undisputed & liquidated. For legal services rendered for my wife and I, at our request. No judgments; no legal action commenced.					100	00
	National City Bank, Steady Credit Dept., Jamaica, N.Y., contracted at Jamaica, N.Y. during 1971; undisputed and liquidated. Personal loan evidenced by promissory note. No judgment; no legal action commenced. Interest and charges due on					397	76
	Mrs. Anna Black, 50 Smith Street, Rye, N.Y., contracted Dec. 1971, at Rye, N.Y.; liquidated & undisputed. Personal loan contracted personally with my wife, Joan Smith. (Mrs. Black is my wife's mother.) No promissory note; no judgment; no legal action commenced.					1,100	00
	Anna Smith, 10 Essex Street, Islip, N.Y., contracted between Aug. 1979 and October, 1972; liquidated & undisputed. As stated on "Statement of Affairs", page 2, paragraph 11, subdivision "a", the debt of $3,500. owed to Mrs. Smith, my mother, was sought to be paid by the transfer to her of said realty. If the transfer is set aside, then I will still owe my mother $3,500.00. No promissory note; no judgment; no legal action commenced.					3,500	00
	Fred Allan, 108 Fourth St., Brooklyn, N.Y.; contracted at Brooklyn, N.Y., September 19, 1971; liquidated & undisputed. For monies due. Judgment dated 6/28/73; transcript docted in Nassau Co. Clk's Office 7/11/73. Contracted with my wife; promissory notes executed by my wife and I.					937	16
	Hempstead Bank, Mineola, L.I., New York; contracted at Mineola, N.Y. during approx. October-November of 1972; liquidated & undisputed. Judgment dated 5/23/73, Supreme Court, Suffolk Co., index #333444, for					5,468	17
	Brooklyn Water Authority, Brooklyn, N.Y.; utility company; dated 11/30/73; liquidated & undisputed; no judgment, promissory note or legal action					6	15
	Consolidated Edison, Huntington, N.Y.; dated 1/9/71; liquidated & undisputed; no judgment, promissory note or legal action.					63	57
	Long Island General Store, Smithtown, N.Y., dated September 8, October 8, 1972; liquidated & undisputed; no judgment, promissory note or legal action; merchandise for store.					34	85
	Grand Art Co., Islip, N.Y., dated 12/5/72; liquidated & undisputed; merchandise for store; no promissory note, no judgment; no legal action commenced.					29	53
	National Cigar Co., L.I.C., N.Y., dated 2/14/72; liquidated & undisputed; merchandise for store; no promissory note, no judgment or legal action commenced.					51	89
					Total	11,689	13

JOHN SMITH   **Petitioner**

1005—Official Form.

JULIUS BLUMBERG, INC., LAW BLANK PUBLISHERS
80 EXCHANGE PLACE, AT BROADWAY, NEW YORK

SCHEDULE A.—STATEMENT OF ALL DEBTS OF DEBTOR (Continued)
Schedule A-4

Liabilities on notes or bills discounted which ought to be paid by the drawers, makers, acceptors, or indorsers.

(N. B.—The dates of the notes or bills, and when due, with the names, residences, and the business or occupation of the drawers, makers, acceptors, or indorsers thereof, are to be set forth under the names of the holders. If the names of the holders are not known, the name of the last holder known to the debtor shall be stated, and his business and place of residence. The same particulars shall be stated as to notes or bills on which the debtor is liable as indorser.)

Reference to ledger or voucher.	Names of holders as far as known.	Residences (if unknown, that fact must be stated.)	Place where contracted.	Whether claim is disputed.	Nature and consideration of liability, whether same was contracted as partner or joint contractor, or with any other person; and, if so, with whom.	Amount due or claimed.	
						$	
	Long Island City Savings Bank	Box 555 Mineola, N.Y.	Mineola, New York	undisputed			
	Mortgage note and mortgage on premises 100 Center Street, Mineola, New York (for premises referred to at paragraph "11", subdivision "a" of the "Statement of Affairs). Mortgage was taken out jointly with my wife at the time we acquired title to the premises on August 6, 1969. The balance presently due on this mortgage, as of August, 1973, is approximately					10,159	00
					Total	10,159	00

_____ JOHN SMITH _____ **Petitioner**

Form 4 *(continued)*

1006—Official Form.

JULIUS BLUMBERG, INC., LAW BLANK PUBLISHERS
80 EXCHANGE PLACE, AT BROADWAY, NEW YORK

SCHEDULE A-5.

Accommodation paper.

(N. B.—The dates of the notes or bills, and when due, with the names and residences of the drawers, makers, acceptors, and indorsers thereof, are to be set forth under the names of the holders; if the debtor be liable as drawer, maker, acceptor, or indorser thereof, it is to be stated accordingly. If the names of the holders are not known, the name of the last holder known to the debtor should be stated, with his residence. Give same particulars as to other commercial paper.)

Reference to ledger or voucher.	Names of holders.	Residences (if unknown, that fact must be stated.)	Names and residences of persons accommodated.	Place where contracted.	Whether claim is disputed.	Whether liability was contracted as partner or joint contractor, or with any other person; and, if so, with whom.	Amount due or claimed.	
	None						$	
						Total	00	00

JOHN SMITH   **Petitioner**

139

JULIUS BLUMBERG, INC., LAW BLANK PUBLISHERS
80 EXCHANGE PLACE, AT BROADWAY, NEW YORK

OATH TO SCHEDULE A.

STATE OF   NEW YORK

COUNTY OF   NASSAU   } ss. :

    I,   JOHN SMITH,

the person who subscribed to the foregoing schedule, do hereby make solemn oath that the said schedule is a statement of all my debts, in accordance with the Act of Congress relating to bankruptcy, according to the best of my knowledge, information, and belief.

....**Petitioner**

     JOHN SMITH

Subscribed and sworn to before me this

1st   day of   November   19 73

....
NOTARY PUBLIC : STATE OF NEW YORK

....

     (Official Character)

This oath may be administered by officers authorized to administer oaths in proceedings before Courts of the United States or under the laws of the State where the same are to be taken; and diplomatic or consular officers of the United States in any foreign country.

Form 4 (continued)

1008—Official Form.

JULIUS BLUMBERG, INC. LAW BLANK PUBLISHERS
80 EXCHANGE PLACE, AT BROADWAY. NEW YORK

SCHEDULE B.—STATEMENT OF ALL PROPERTY OF DEBTOR

Schedule B-1.

Real Estate

Location and description of all real estate owned by debtor, or held by him, whether under deed, lease or contract.	Incumbrances thereon, if any, and dates thereof.	Statement of particulars relating thereto.	Estimated value of debtor's interest.	
NONE			$ 00	00
			00	00
		Total..........	00	00

JOHN SMITH _____ **Petitioner**

141

Form 4 *(continued)*

1009—Official Form.

JULIUS BLUMBERG INC. LAW BLANK PUBLISHERS
80 EXCHANGE PLACE AT BROADWAY, NEW YORK

SCHEDULE B-2.   *Personal property.*

				$	
a Cash on hand.	$3.00			?	00
b Negotiable and non-negotiable instruments, and securities of any description, including stocks in incorporated companies, interests in joint stock companies, and the like (each to be set out separately.)	None			00	00
c Stock in trade, in business of · at · of the value of	None			00	00
d Household goods and furniture, household stores, wearing apparel and ornaments of the person. owned jointly with wife Joan Smith	2 sets dishes 4 beds, studio couch coach, 2 chairs television set 2 end tables 2 lamps	kitchen table 4 kitchen chairs fish tank 1 night table 1 lamp 1 dishwasher	1 refrigerator desk chest 3 suits 1 projector camera	200	00
e Books, prints, and pictures.	20 novels 1 set encyclopedia (mixed)			5	00
f Horses, cows, sheep, and other animals (with number of each).	None			00	00
g Automobiles and other vehicles.	1956 Chevrolet			25	00
h Farming stock and implements of husbandry.	None			00	00
i Shipping, and shares in vessels.	None			00	00
j Machinery, fixtures, apparatus, and tools used in business, with the place where each is situated.	Hammer, saw, plane, pliers, screw driver, miscellaneous hand tools, lawn mower, hose, garden tools			50	00
k Patents, copy-rights, and trade-marks.	None			00	00
l Goods or personal property of any other description, with the place where each is situated.	None			00	00
			Total	283	00

JOHN SMITH   *Petitioner*

142

1010—Official Form.

JULIUS BLUMBERG, INC., LAW BLANK PUBLISHERS
80 EXCHANGE PLACE, AT BROADWAY, NEW YORK

SCHEDULE B.—STATEMENT OF ALL PROPERTY OF DEBTOR (Continued)
Schedule B-3.

Choses in action.

a Debts due petitioner on open account.		$	
	Della Smith of 111 Second Street, Mineola, L.I., N.Y., holds $300.00 of security paid by me pursuant to clause 27 of a lease dated September 19, 1971, with reference to the store where I conducted the business known as Mineola Stationery.	300	00
	Total............	300	00

JOHN SMITH   𝔓𝔢𝔱𝔦𝔱𝔦𝔬𝔫𝔢𝔯

Form 4 (continued)

1012—Official Form.

JULIUS BLUMBERG, INC., LAW BLANK PUBLISHERS
80 EXCHANGE PLACE AT BROADWAY, NEW YORK

SCHEDULE B-4.

Property in reversion, remainder, or expectancy, including property held in trust for the debtor or subject to any power or right to dispose of or to charge.

(N. B.—A particular description of each interest must be entered, with a statement of the location of the property, the names and description of the persons now enjoying the same, the value thereof, and from whom and in what manner debtor's interest in such property is or will be derived. If all or any of the debtor's property has been conveyed by deed of assignment, or otherwise, for the benefit of creditors, the date of such deed should be stated, the name and address of the person to whom the property was conveyed, the amount realized as the proceeds thereof, and the disposal of the same, as far as known to the debtor.)

GENERAL INTEREST.	PARTICULAR DESCRIPTION	Estimated value of interest.	
Interest in land.	None	00	00
Personal property.	None	00	00
Property in money, stock, shares, bonds, annuities, etc.	None	00	00
Rights and powers, legacies and bequests.	None	00	00
	Total	00	00
PROPERTY HERETOFORE CONVEYED FOR BENEFIT OF CREDITORS. Portion of debtor's property conveyed by deed of assignment, or otherwise, for the benefit of creditors; date of such deed, name and address of party to whom conveyed; amount realized therefrom, and disposal of same, as far as known to debtor.	None	Amount realized as proceeds of property conveyed.	
		000	00
ATTORNEY'S FEES. Sum or sums paid to counsel, and to whom, for services rendered or to be rendered in this bankruptcy.	Paid in full to Joe Attorney for attorney's fees	200	00
	Paid in full to Joe Attorney for filing fees	50	00
	(Both paid by John Smith)		
	Total	250	00

_____ **Petitioner**

Form 4 (*continued*)

1013—Official Form.

JULIUS BLUMBERG, INC., LAW BLANK PUBLISHERS
80 EXCHANGE PLACE, AT BROADWAY, NEW YORK

SCHEDULE B.—STATEMENT OF ALL PROPERTY OF DEBTOR (Continued)

Schedule B-5.

Property claimed as exempt from the operation of the act of Congress relating to bankruptcy.

(N. B.—Each item of property must be stated, with its valuation, and, if any portion of it is real estate, its location description and present use.)

Property claimed to be	Description	Valuation	
Property claimed to be exempt by the laws of the United States, with reference to the statute creating the exemption.	Miscellaneous hand tools (hammer, saw, screw driver, plane, pliers, etc.), lawn mower, hose, garden tools	$ 50	00
	20 novels, i set encyclopedia (mixed)	5	00
	2 sets dishes, 4 beds, studio couch, couch, 2 chairs, television set, 2 end tables, 2 lamps, kitchen table, 4 kitchen chairs, fish tank, 1 night table, 1 lamp, 1 dishwasher, 1 refrigerator, desk, chest, 3 suits, 1 projector camera	200	00
Property claimed to be exempt by State laws, with reference to the statute creating the exemption.	Miscellaneous hand tools (hammer, saw, screw driver, plane, pliers, etc.), lawn mower, hose, garden tools	50	00
	20 novels, 1 set encyclopedia (mixed)	5	00
	2 sets dishes, 4 beds, studio couch, couch, 2 chairs, television set, 2 end tables, 2 lamps, kitchen table, 4 kitchen chairs, fish tank, 1 night table, 1 lamp, 1 dishwasher, 1 refrigerator, desk, chest, 3 suits, 1 projector camera	200	00
	Total	255	00

JOHN SMITH

Petitioner

145

1014—Official Form.

JULIUS BLUMBERG, INC. LAW BLANK PUBLISHERS
80 EXCHANGE PLACE, AT BROADWAY. NEW YORK

SCHEDULE B-6.

Books, papers, deeds and writings relating to debtor's business and estate.

The following is a true list of all books, papers, deeds and writings relating to petitioner's trade, business, dealings, estate and effects, or any part thereof, which, at the date of this petition, are in petitioner's possession or under petitioner's custody and control, or which are in the possession or custody of any person in trust for petitioner, or for petitioner's use, benefit, or advantage; and also of all others which have been heretofore, at any time, in petitioner's possession, or under petitioner's custody or control, and which are now held by the parties whose names are hereinafter set forth, with the reason for their custody of the same.

Books	Two: One for Mineola Stationery and one for X Y Z Floor Waxing Service, in my possession at 100 Center Street, Mineola, N.Y.
Deeds	None
Papers	Copies of Federal and State Income Tax Returns and bank papers in my possession at 100 Center Street, Mineola, New York. Miscellaneous papers from the 2 businesses in my possession at 100 Center Street, Mineola, New York.

JOHN SMITH   Petitioner

JULIUS BLUMBERG, INC., LAW BLANK PUBLISHERS
80 EXCHANGE PLACE, AT BROADWAY, NEW YORK

OATH TO SCHEDULE B.

STATE OF   NEW YORK

COUNTY OF   NASSAU   } ss.:

   I,   JOHN SMITH,

the person who subscribed to the foregoing schedule, do hereby make solemn oath that the said schedule is a statement of all my property, real and personal, in accordance with the Act of Congress relating to bankruptcy, according to the best of my knowledge, information, and belief.

....Petitioner

      JOHN SMITH

Subscribed and sworn to before me this

1st   day of   November   19 73

....

NOTARY PUBLIC : STATE OF NEW YORK
....
(*Official Character*)

This oath may be administered by officers authorized to administer oaths in proceedings before Courts of the United States or under the laws of the State where the same are to be taken; and diplomatic or consular officers of the United States in any foreign country.

Form 4 (*continued*)

1016—Official Form.

JULIUS BLUMBERG, INC., LAW BLANK PUBLISHERS
80 EXCHANGE PLACE, AT BROADWAY, NEW YORK

SUMMARY OF DEBTS AND ASSETS

(From the statements of the debtor in Schedule A and B.)

			$	
Schedule A	1-a	Wages.	00	00
Schedule A	1-b (1)	Taxes due United States.	00	00
Schedule A	1-b (2)	Taxes due States.	00	00
Schedule A	1-b (3)	Taxes due counties, districts and municipalities.	00	00
Schedule A	1-c (1)	Debts due any person, including the United States, having priority by laws of the United States.	00	00
Schedule A	1-c (2)	Rent having priority.	00	00
Schedule A	2	Secured claims.	00	00
Schedule A	3	Unsecured claims.	11,689	13
Schedule A	4	Notes and bills which ought to be paid by other parties thereto.	10,159	00
Schedule A	5	Accommodation paper.	00	00
		Schedule A, Total	21,848	13
Schedule B	1	Real estate.	$ 00	00
Schedule B	2-a	Cash on hand.	3	00
Schedule B	2-b	Negotiable and non-negotiable instruments and securities.	00	00
Schedule B	2-c	Stock in trade.	00	00
Schedule B	2-d	Household goods.	00	00
Schedule B	2-e	Books, prints, and pictures.	00	00
Schedule B	2-f	Horses, cows, and other animals.	00	00
Schedule B	2-g	Automobiles and other vehicles.	25	00
Schedule B	2-h	Farming stock and implements.	00	00
Schedule B	2-i	Shipping and shares in vessels.	00	00
Schedule B	2-j	Machinery, fixtures, and tools.	50	00
Schedule B	2-k	Patents, copyrights, and trade-marks.	00	00
Schedule B	2-l	Other personal property.	00	00
Schedule B	3-a	Debts due on open accounts.	300	00
Schedule B	3-b	Policies of insurance.	00	00
Schedule B	3-c	Unliquidated claims.	00	00
Schedule B	3-d	Deposits of money in banks and elsewhere.	00	00
Schedule B	4	Property in reversion, remainder, expectancy or trust.	00	00
Schedule B	5	Property claimed as exempt.	00	00
Schedule B	6	Books, deeds and papers.	00	00
		Schedule B, Total	378	00

JOHN SMITH   *Petitioner*

148

Form 5   Sample of Order of Discharge of Bankrupt

BK-45 (11-70)

United States District Court

for the EASTERN   . . . .   District of . NEW YORK . . . .

IN THE MATTER OF

        JOHN SMITH

                 Bankrupt.

IN BANKRUPTCY

NO. ___ . . . .

ORDER OF
DISCHARGE OF BANKRUPT

It appearing that the person named above was duly adjudged a bankrupt on a petition filed on JANUARY 10, 1974 , and that no objection to the discharge of the bankrupt was filed within the time fixed by the court [or that objections to the discharge of the bankrupt were filed and, after due notice and hearing, were not sustained]; it is ordered that

   1. the above-named bankrupt is released from all dischargeable debts;

   2. any judgment heretofore or hereafter obtained in any court other than this court is null and void as a determination of the personal liability of the bankrupt with respect to any of the following:
     (a) debts not excepted from the discharge under § 17a or § 17b of the Bankruptcy Act;
     (b) debts discharged under § 17c(2) of the Bankruptcy Act; and
     (c) debts determined to be discharged under § 17c(3) of the Bankruptcy Act; and

   3. all creditors whose debts are discharged by this order are enjoined from instituting or continuing any action or employing any process to collect such debts as personal liabilities of the bankrupt above named.

Dated: JAMAICA, N.Y.
        JANUARY, 1974

                                     Referee in Bankruptcy

- -

Certified copies of the Order of Discharge may be obtained from the Referee in Bankruptcy or, if case is closed, from the Clerk of Court for registration in other districts.

IPI NI—II 8 76 JN PADS 5561

Form 6   Sample of Petition Filed Under Chapter XIII*

IN THE DISTRICT COURT OF THE UNITED STATES
FOR THE SOUTHERN DISTRICT OF NEW YORK

IN THE MATTER OF

_____JOE DEBTOR, DEBTOR

In proceedings for a
Wage Earner Plan under
Chapter XIII

No.....................

PETITION

TO THE HONORABLE JUDGE

JUDGE OF THE DISTRICT COURT OF THE UNITED STATES
FOR THE SOUTHERN DISTRICT OF NEW YORK.

The petition of JOE DEBTOR, Social Security No. 296-2000-

300, residing at 1111 12th Avenue, New York City, a Teacher by

occupation and employed by ALLIED COLLEGE respectfully represents:

1.   Your petitioner is an individual whose principal
income is derived from wages, salary or commission.

2.   No bankruptcy proceeding initiated by a petition by or
against your petitioner is now pending.

3.   Your petitioner is unable to pay his debts as they
mature, and desires to effect an extension of time to pay his
debts out of his future earnings.

4.   The schedule hereto annexed, marked Schedule A, contains a full and true statement of all his debts and, so far as it is
possible to ascertain, the names and places of residence of his creditors, and such further statements concerning said debts as are
required by the provisions of the Act of Congress relating to
Bankruptcy.

5.   The schedule hereto annexed, marked Schedule B, contains a full and true and accurate inventory of all his property,
real and personal, and a full and complete statement of affairs and
of executory contracts, as required by the provisions of said Act.

WHEREFORE, your Petitioner prays that proceedings may be had
upon this Petition in accordance with the provisions of Chapter XIII
of the Act of Congress relating to Bankruptcy.

```
                                        _____
                                        PETITIONER
A. Good
_____
Attorney

STATE OF NEW YORK  )
COUNTY OF NEW YORK )  SS:
```

I, a Debtor in the within described proceedings, who subscribed to the foregoing document, do hereby make solemn oath that
the statements contained therein and in the attached documents are
true and complete according to the best of my knowledge, information
and belief.

```
                                        _____
                                        Debtor
```
Sworn and subscribed to before me this 20 day of October, 1973.
My Commission expires

* NOTE: Except for the first page shown above, the petition filed under Chapter
XIII is similar to that filed for "straight" bankruptcy. Therefore, the form of
Schedules for a Chapter XIII petition is not included here. It is to be noted,
however, that all property exemptions are waived in a Chapter XIII proceeding.

Form 7 Sample of Notice to Creditors Under Chapter XIII

UNITED STATES DISTRICT COURT
EASTERN DISTRICT OF NEW YORK
- - - - - - - - - - - - - -x

In the Matter of: No.

   THOMAS J.----

                 Debtor.
For relief under Chapter XIII
Sec. 622 of the Bankruptcy Act.
- - - - - - - - - - - - - - -x

TO THE CREDITORS OF THOMAS J.-----------,   Adams Boulevard,
               Flushing, N.Y. in the County of Queens,
               and district aforesaid:

On April 20, 1972 the said debtor filed a petition in this Court
stating that he desires to effect a composition or an extension
of time to pay his debts out of his future earnings and praying
that proceedings be had upon his petition in accordance with the
provisions of Chapter XIII of the Bankruptcy Act.

NOTICE IS HEREBY GIVEN that a Meeting of creditors will be held
in Room 502, 92-32 Union Hall Street, Jamaica, New York on May
18, 1972 at 10:30 a.m. and at that place and time the debtor
shall submit his plan of payment and the said creditors may
attend, prove their claims, examine the debtor on any matter
relevant to the proceeding, present written acceptances of the
plan proposed, and transact such other business as may properly
come before said meeting. The debtor may obtain the written
acceptances of creditors which shall be presented to the Court
at that meeting.

NOTICE IS ALSO HEREBY GIVEN that at said meeting on May 18, 1972
the application to confirm said plan, if accepted, shall be filed
with this Court and a hearing on confirmation and objections,
thereto, if any, will be held at that time then said hearing may
be adjourned, or the proceeding dismissed, of if he consents, the
debtor may be adjudicated a bankrupt.

Debtor's attorney shall file his application for fee and expenses
at or before said meeting.

Distribution of payments will be made only to creditors who have
filed their claims on or before November 17, 1972. Proof of claim
must be filed at the address below whether or not the creditor
is included in the schedules of the debtor.

    LAST DAY FOR FILING CLAIMS: NOVEMBER 17, 1972

Notify Referee's office promptly of any change in claimant's post
office address.

EACH CREDITOR FILING A CLAIM SHALL ANNEX THERETO A STATMENT THAT
SUCH CLAIM IS FREE FROM USURY AS DEFINED BY THE LAWS OF THE PLACE
WHERE THE DEBT WAS CONTRACTED.

Dated at Jamaica, N.Y.
    May 8, 1972   Referee in Bankruptcy
                              92-32 Union Hall Street
                              Jamaica, N.Y. 11433

Form 8   Sample of Proposed Plan for Payment Under Chapter XIII

UNITED STATES DISTRICT COURT
EASTERN DISTRICT OF NEW YORK

In the Matter of
          John Doe   In Proceedings for a
                                      Wage Earner Plan
          Debtor.   No.

PLAN.

John Doe, the above named debtor, proposes the following plan:

ARTICLE 1.

PROVISIONS DEALING WITH UNSECURED DEBTS.

(A)   The unsecured debts of the debtor shall be settled and satisfied by the full payment to the holders thereof of their respective debts, but the time for payment of said debts shall be extended so that said debts shall be payable out of monies to be paid by the debtor under subdivision (B) of the Article.

(B)   The debtor shall pay out of his future earnings or wages the sum of $20.00 (Twenty) Dollars on Monday of each week commencing with the first Monday following confirmation of this plan. Said installment payments shall be made by the debtor to the trustee appointed herein to receive and distribute all moneys to be paid under the plan. From the moneys paid to said trustee, there shall be made the payments required by the provisions of section 659 of Chapter XIII of the Bankruptcy Act, the said payments to unsecured creditors, and all other payments provided for in this plan. The installment payments by the debtor to the trustee shall continue until the debtor shall have paid the total moneys required for such distribution by said trustee.

ARTICLE II.

PROVISIONS DEALING WITH SECURED DEBTS

(A)   First National Bank, the holder of a claim against the debtor for $180.00 secured by a security interest in an automobile of the debtor, shall be paid in full, but the time for payment of said debts shall be extended so that said debt shall be payable out of the moneys to be paid by the debtor under Article I.

(B)   The Fulton Savings Bank, the holder of a claim against the debtor for $21,550.00, secured by a mortgage on a house owned by debtor at 1000 Adams Avenue, Queens, New York, shall not be included in the plan but shall be paid by the debtor outside the plan.

ARTICLE III.

PROVISIONS FOR PRIORITY OF PAYMENT

There shall be no priority of payment during the period of extension as between the secured and unsecured debts affected by the plan.

ARTICLE IV.

PROVISIONS FOR SUBMISSION OF FUTURE EARNINGS OR WAGES

The future earnings and wages of the debtor are submitted to the supervision and control of the court for the purpose of enforcing the plan.

ARTICLE V

PROVISIONS FOR INCREASING OR REDUCING INSTALLMENT PAYMENTS, OR EXTENDING OR SHORTENING THE TIME THEREFOR.

The court may from time to time during the period of extension increase or reduce the amount of any of the installment payments provided by the plan, or extend or shorten the time for any such payments, where it shall be made to appear, after hearing upon such notice as the court may designate, that the circumstances of the debtor so warrant or require.

Form 8 (*continued*)

ARTICLE VI.

PROVISIONS FOR THE REJECTION OF EXECUTORY CONTRACTS

There do not presently exist any executory contracts which the debtor requests rejection.

ARTICLE VII.

GENERAL PROVISIONS.

In the event the indebtness of the debtor for money borrowed or for merchandise purchased on credit subsequent to the filing of his petition to effect a plan shall at any time exceed one hundred ($100) Dollars, this plan shall thereupon terminate.

Dated: New York, New York, January 25, 1974

_____

JOHN DOE, Debtor.

Form 9 Sample of Voluntary Bankruptcy Petition Under Chapter XI

In the District Court of the United States for the   Eastern   District of   New York

In the matter of

John Doe, doing business as

Ace Movers

In Proceedings
for an Arrangement

No....................

See footnote   Debtor

PETITION IN PROCEEDINGS UNDER CHAPTER XI

To the Honorable Judges of the District Court of the United States

for the   Eastern   District of   New York

THE PETITION of John Doe, doing business as Ace Movers

of   1234 Main Street, New York City, New York

a corporation engaged in the business of   Trucking

which corporation has not been known by any name or trade name for the past six years, other than as set forth in the above caption,

RESPECTFULLY REPRESENTS:

USE IF
PETI-
TIONER
IS A
CORP-
ORATION

1. Your petitioner is a [moneyed, business or commercial] *corporation organized and existing under the laws of the State of New York   and has had its principal office and its principal place of business at   1234 Main Street   within the above judicial district, for the six months immediately preceding the filing of this petition [or for a longer portion of the six months immediately preceding the filing of this petition than in any other judicial district].

2. †No bankruptcy proceeding, initiated by a petition by or against your petitioner, is now pending.

[OR, IF APPROPRIATE, STRIKE OUT SENTENCE ABOVE AND REPLACE WITH: Petitioner was adjudicated a bankrupt in 19____ (more than 6 years ago)]

3. Your petitioner is insolvent [or unable to pay its debts as they mature], and proposes the following arrangement with its unsecured creditors:

[or intends to propose an arrangement pursuant to the provisions of Chapter XI of the Bankruptcy Act.]

NOTE: Set forth in caption all assumed, trade and any other names or designations by or under which bankrupt or debtor has been known or has conducted any business within preceding 6 years.
*Moneyed, Business or Commercial.
†If Bankruptcy proceeding is pending and this petition is brought under Chapter XI, Section 321, strike out this allegation and recite proceedings heretofore had.

155

4. The schedule hereto annexed, marked Schedule A, and verified by the oath of the undersigned officer of your petitioner, contains a full and true statement of all its debts, and, so far as it is possible to ascertain, the names and places of residence or of business of its creditors, and such further statements concerning its debts as are required by the provisions of the Bankruptcy Act.

5. The schedule hereto annexed, marked Schedule B, and verified by the oath of the undersigned officer of your petitioner, contains an accurate inventory of all its property, real and personal, and such further statements concerning its property as are required by the provisions of the Act.

6. The statement hereto annexed, marked Exhibit 1, and verified by the oath of the undersigned officer of your petitioner, contains a full and true statement of all its executory contracts, as required by the provisions of the Act.

7. The statement hereto annexed, marked Exhibit 2, and verified by the oath of the undersigned officer of your petitioner, contains a full and true statement of its affairs, as required by the provisions of the Act.

WHEREFORE your petitioner prays that proceedings may be had upon this petition in accordance with the provisions of chapter XI of the Bankruptcy Act.

[S]   John Doe
_____
                          Petitioner

By _____

(SEAL)   [USED IF   [TITLE] _____ of said corporation
         PETITIONER
         IS A   Petitioner's Address __1234 Main Street__
         CORPORATION]
                          __New York City, New York__

                          [S]   Joseph Attorney
                          _____
                                        Attorney

                          __567 Main Street, New York City, New York__
                                        Address

STATE OF   New York   ⎫
                       ⎬ ss.:
COUNTY OF New York   ⎭

    John Doe   being duly sworn deposes and says that he is the
[TITLE]   of Ace Movers
the petitioner named in the foregoing petition, and does hereby make solemn oath that the statements contained therein are true, according to the best of his knowledge, information and belief; that the reason why this verification is made by deponent and not by the petitioner herein, is that said petitioner is a corporation; and that deponent is the officer of said corporation duly authorized by its Board of Directors to execute and verify said petition on its behalf.

Subscribed and sworn to before me this
        day of   19   [S]   John Doe
                                      ....

....

....
            (*Official Character*)

NOTE: SCHEDULES SIMILAR TO THOSE USED FOR A STRAIGHT BANKRUPTCY PETITION MUST ACCOMPANY THIS PETITION, AS WELL AS A STATEMENT OF THE DEBTOR'S EXECUTORY CONTRACTS.

277—General Assignment for Benefit of Creditors.
With or Without Preferences.   W   JULIUS BLUMBERG, INC., LAW BLANK PUBLISHERS
80 EXCHANGE PLACE AT BROADWAY, NEW YORK

This Indenture,

Made the day of *in the year one thousand*
nine hundred and
BETWEEN

having *principal place of business at*

part *of the first part*
and
part *of the second part*

WITNESSETH:

WHEREAS *the part* *of the first part ha* *carried on and now* *engaged in the*
business of
at No.

WHEREAS *the part* *of the first part* *indebted to divers persons in sundry sums of*
money, which *unable to pay in full, and* *desirous of pro-*
viding for the payment of the same, so far as it is possible by a general assignment of all
property for that purpose:

NOW, THEREFORE, *the part* *of the first part, in consideration of the premises and of the*
sum of one dollar paid by the part *of the second part, upon the ensealing and delivery of these*
presents, the receipt whereof is hereby acknowledged, ha *granted, bargained, sold, assigned, trans-*
ferred and set over, and by these presents do *grant, bargain, sell, assign, transfer and set over, unto*
the part *of the second part* *successors and assigns, all and singular the lands, tenements,*
hereditaments, appurtenances, goods, chattels, stock, promissory notes, claims, demands, property and
effects of every description belonging to the part *of the first part, wherever the same may be,*
except such property as is exempt by law from levy and sale under an execution.

TO HAVE AND TO HOLD *the same, and every part thereof, unto the said part* *of the*
second part, *successors and assigns.*

IN TRUST, NEVERTHELESS, *to take possession of the same, and to sell the same with all*
reasonable dispatch, and to convert the same into money, and also to collect all such debts and demands
hereby assigned as may be collectible, and out of all the proceeds of such sales and collections, to pay
and discharge all the just and reasonable expenses, costs and disbursements in connection with the execu-
tion of this assignment and the discharge of the trust hereby created, together with the lawful com-
missions or allowances of the part *of the second part for* *services in executing said*
trust; THEN

Form 10 *(continued)*

AND then to pay and discharge in full, if the residue of said proceeds is sufficient for that purpose, all the debts and liabilities now due or to grow due from the said part   of the first part, with all interest moneys due or to grow due thereon; and if the residue of said proceeds shall not be sufficient to pay the said debts and liabilities and interest thereon in full, then to apply the said residue of said proceeds to the payment of said debts and liabilities ratably and in proportion.

AND if, after the payment of all the said debts and liabilities in full, there shall be any remainder or residue of said property or proceeds, to repay and return the same to the said part   of the first part,   executors, administrators or assigns.

AND, in furtherance of the premises, the said part   of the first part do   hereby make, constitute and appoint the said part   of the second part   true and lawful attorney , irrevocable, with full power and authority to do all acts and things which may be necessary in the premises to the full execution of the trust hereby created, and to ask, demand, recover and receive of and from all and every person or persons all property, debts and demands due, owing and belonging to the said part   of the first part, and to give acquittances and discharges for the same; to sue, prosecute, defend and implead for the same; and to execute, acknowledge, and deliver all necessary deeds, instruments and conveyances: and for any of the purposes aforesaid to make, constitute and appoint one or more attorneys under him and at his pleasure to revoke the said appointments, hereby ratifying and confirming whatever the said part   of the second part or   substitutes shall lawfully do in the premises.

AND the said part   of the first part hereby authorize   the said part   of the second part to sign the name   of the said part   of the first part to any check, draft, promissory note or other instrument in writing which is payable to the order of the said part   of the first part, or to sign the name of the part   of the first part to any instrument in writing, whenever it shall be necessary so to do, to carry into effect the object, design and purpose of this trust.

THE said part   of the second part do   hereby accept the trust created and reposed in   by this instrument, and covenant   and agree   to and with the said part   of the first part that   will faithfully and without delay execute the said trust, according to the best of skill, knowledge and ability.

IN WITNESS WHEREOF, the parties hereto have hereunto set their hands and seals the day and year first above written.

....
Assignor

....
Assignee

Form 10 *(continued)*

STATE OF

COUNTY OF $\Big\}$ ss.:

    On the   day of   , nineteen hundred and
before me came

to me known and known to me to be the individual   described in, and who executed, the foregoing instrument, and acknowledged to me that   he   executed the same.

STATE OF

COUNTY OF $\Big\}$ ss.:

    On the   day of   , nineteen hundred and
before me came
                                            to me known, who,
being by me duly sworn, did depose and say that   he resides in

that   he is the   of

the corporation described in, and which executed, the foregoing instrument; that   he knows the seal of said corporation; that the seal affixed to said instrument is such corporate seal; that it was so affixed by order of the board of   of said corporation; and that   he signed h name thereto by like order.

Form 11   Sample Form of Questions
Asked by Judgment Creditors of Debtors

W 451—Questions: spaces for judgment debtor to
answer—use with information subpoena
(Blumbergs No. 407 or 417). Blank Ct.:   4-64

COPYRIGHT 1964 BY JULIUS BLUMBERG, INC., LAW BLANK PUBLISHERS
80 EXCHANGE PLACE AT BROADWAY, NEW YORK

CIVIL   COURT OF THE CITY OF NEW YORK
COUNTY OF   QUEENS

Index No.

CHARLES DEBTOR,

                                                        Plaintiff

                    against

DAVID DEBTOR,

                                                        Defendant

QUESTIONS AND ANSWERS
in connection with
INFORMATION SUBPOENA
regarding

Judgment Debtor

STATE OF NEW YORK, COUNTY OF   ss.:

                    DAVID DEBTOR   being duly sworn deposes and says; that deponent is
the * Judgment Debtor above named and the recipient of an information subpoena herein and of the original and a
copy of questions accompanying said subpoena. Deponent makes the following answers (each answer immediately
following the question to which it responds) in compliance with the subpoena.

1. Q. What is your full name? A.
2. Q. Have you ever been known by any other name? A.
3. Q. What is your occupation or profession? A.
4. Q. Where do you live and with whom? A.

5. Q. Do you occupy an apartment or house? A.
6. Q. What is the landlord's name and address? A.

7. Q. Have you a written lease? A.
8. Q. Who pays the rent? A.
9. Q. How is the rent paid, by check or cash? A.
10. Q. When is the rent payable? A.
11. Q. Do you get receipts for the rent from your landlord? A.
12. Q. How much is the rent? A.
13. Q. For how long a time have you lived in the premises you now occupy? A.
14. Q. How much security do you have on deposit with your landlord? A.
15. Q. Are you married? A.
16. Q. What is your spouse's full name? A.
17. Q. Are you the owner of the household furnishings in your home? A.
18. Q. Did you buy said furnishings on the installment plan? A.
19. Q. Are said furnishings covered by a security agreement such as a chattel mortgage or conditional sale contract?
        A.
20. Q. Are said furnishings insured? A.
21. Q. If so, in whose name, and in what company? A.

22. Q. How many children have you, and what are their ages? A.

23. Q. Are any of your children employed? A.
24. Q. Is your spouse engaged in an independent business? A.
25. Q. What is the name and address of the business? A.

26. Q. What is the nature of the business? A.
27. Q. Is your spouse employed? A.
28. Q. What is the name and address of the employer? A.

29. Q. What is the nature of the occupation? A.
30. Q. What salary is paid to your spouse? A.
31. Q. Does your spouse own any real estate or have any interest in real estate? A.

32. Q. Does your spouse hold any chattel mortgages or security agreements? A.

33. Q. Does your spouse own an automobile, airplane or boat? A.
34. Q. Is the same covered by a chattel mortgage, conditional sale or other security agreement? A.

35. Q. Has your spouse a bank, check or savings account? A.

36. Q. Has your spouse any jewelry? A.
37. Q. Describe each item of jewelry and give approximate values? A.

* Excerpt from CPLR section 5224 (a) 3. ". . . . . . Answers shall be made in writing under oath by the person upon whom served, if an
individual, or by an officer, director, agent or employee having information, if a corporation, partnership or sole proprietorship. Each question
shall be answered separately and fully and each answer shall refer to the question to which it responds. Answers shall be returned together
with the original of the questions within seven days after receipt." If space is insufficient, use last page to answer, giving number of the
question answered.

38. Q. Is your spouse an officer, director or stockholder in any corporation? A.

39. Q. Does your spouse own any stocks, bonds, defense bonds or other securities? A.
40. Q. Identify each such item? A.

41. Q. Are any of your children officers, directors or stockholders in any corporation? A.

42. Q. Are you engaged in business in an individual, partnership or corporate form? A.

43. Q. If engaged in business give your business address and name of your firm? A.

44. Q. If employed give your employer's name and address? A.

45. Q. What share or interest have you in the firm with which you are connected? A.
46. Q. In what capacity are you employed? A.
47. Q. Are you employed under a written contract? A.
48. Q. For how long a time have you worked with your present employer? A.
49. Q. What salary do you receive? A.
50. Q. When is your salary payable? A.
51. Q. Is your salary payable by check or in cash? A.
52. Q. Do you receive any bonus or emolument other than your salary? A.
53. Q. Have you a drawing account? A.
54. Q. What amount of income have you received from your trade or profession during each of the two years immediately preceding the entry of judgment in this action? A.
55. Q. What amount of income have you received from other sources during each of these two years? A.

56. Q. Have you a bank, check or savings account? A.
57. Q. If so, give names and addresses of banks where you have accounts? A.

58. Q. Have you closed any bank account since the summons in this action was served on you? A.

59. Q. If so give name and address of bank. A.

60. Q. How much was on deposit at time the account was closed? A.

61. Q. Give date, name and address of payee of the last check you drew. A.

62. Q. What was the amount of said check and the consideration therefor? A.

63. Q. Is the payee related to you, or to any member of your family? A.
64. Q. Have you any life, accident, health or any other kind of insurance? A.
65. Q. If so, what are the names of the companies and the numbers and amounts of each policy? A.

66. Q. Who are the beneficiaries in each policy? A.

67. Q. Were the beneficiaries changed? If so, when? A.
68. Q. Do you own an automobile, airplane or boat? A.
69. Q. Is it covered by a chattel mortgage, conditional sale or other security agreement? A.

70. Q. Was it bought on the installment plan? A.
71. Q. Where do you keep the automobile? A.
72. Q. Have you any jewelry or diamonds? A.
73. Q. Describe each item and give approximate values? A.

74. Q. Do you own any interest in real estate? A.

75. Q. Do you have shares or proprietory lease in a cooperative or condominium? A.

76. Q. Do you own any chattel or real estate mortgages? A.

77. Q. Do you hold any participating interest in any real estate or chattel mortgage? A.

78. Q. Do you receive any income from trust funds? A.

79. Q. Do you own any stocks, bonds, defense bonds or other securities? A.
80. Q. Describe each item? A.

81. Q. Are you an officer, director or shareholder in any corporation? A.

82. Q. Do you own a piano, phonograph, radio, television set, horses, carriages, trucks, paintings or silverware? A.

83. Q. Do you own any rugs or tapestries? If so, describe them. *A.*

84. Q. Have you a library, collection of curios, coins, stamps, antiques or statuary? *A.*

85. Q. Do you receive royalties from any patent, copyright or invention? *A.*

86. Q. Do you own a seat in any stock, cotton, produce, commercial or other exchange? *A.*

87. Q. Are you a trustee, executor or administrator under any will or testament, insurance policy or trust agreement? *A.*

88. Q. Have you any property in pawn? *A.*

89. Q. Did you ever borrow money and pledge or deposit as collateral security any property, real or personal? *A.*

90. Q. If so, state names and addresses of persons with whom such security was deposited. *A.*

91. Q. Have you made a last will and testament? *A.*
92. Q. Have you one or more safe deposit boxes? *A.*
93. Q. If so, give the location of each and the names of all persons having access to each box? *A.*

94. Q. Do you have access to any other safe deposit box? *A.*

95. Q. Are you a beneficiary under any trust or last will? *A.*

96. Q. Are you a lessee of any real estate? *A.*
97. Q. If so, where is the property located. *A.*

98. Q. Have you an interest in any mortgage, mechanics lien or other lien on real property? *A.*

99. Q. Have you any judgments in your favor? *A.*
100. Q. If so, state details and amounts. *A.*

101. Q. Does anybody owe you money? *A.*
102. Q. If so, give details? *A.*

103. Q. Are there any judgments against you? *A.*
104. Q. If so, state details and amounts. *A.*

105. Q. Have you ever before been examined by a judgment creditor? *A.*

106. Q. Have you any right or interest in any action now pending in any court? *A.*

107. Q. Are you a party to any action now pending in any court? *A.*

108. Q. Have you sold, conveyed or assigned any of your property real or personal within the past 2 years? *A.*

109. Q. Have you made a gift of any of your real or personal property to anyone since the summons in the above entitled action was served on you? *A.*

110. Q. Are you named as beneficiary under a life insurance policy issued to some other person? *A.*

111. Q. Have you received any money or property under any will or by inheritance? *A.*

112. Q. Was a receiver of your property ever appointed? *A.*

113. Q. How do you pay for your living expenses? *A.*

114. Q. What is the source of your income which you use to support yourself? *A.*

115. Q. Do you receive any money from others to help support yourself? *A.*
116. Q. If so, give names and addresses of such persons. *A.*

117. Q. Give the amounts that such persons contribute for your support. *A.*

118. Q. Do you receive such monies by check or in cash? *A.*
119. Q. What deposits have you with any utility company? *A.*

Form 11 *(continued)*

120. Q. Do you receive or are you entitled to receive money from trust or pension funds? *A.*

121. Q. Have you any sources of income other than as testified to? *A.*

122. Q. Where did you file your Federal and State income tax returns for the past 2 years? *A.*

123. Q. Are you entitled to any refund for Federal or State income taxes paid? *A.*

124. Q. Does anyone hold any property or money in trust for you? *A.*

125. Q. Do you keep any records relating to your income and expenses? *A.*
126. Q. Do you employ an accountant? *A.*
127. Q. Have you borrowed money from any bank or other lending institution within the past 2 years? *A.*

128. Q. Do you have an interest in insurance or other claims now pending? *A.*
129. Q. If so, give details? *A.*

Form 12   Sample of Subpoena
and Restraining Notice Used for Debtor or Third Party

X 410 -- Information Subpoena with RESTRAINING NOTICE: to Garnishee-Witness; Enforcement of Money Judgments: Civil Court.

COPYRIGHT 1966 BY JULIUS BLUMBERG, INC., LAW BLANK PUBLISHERS
80 EXCHANGE PLACE AT BROADWAY, NEW YORK

CIVIL COURT OF THE CITY OF NEW YORK
COUNTY OF

Index No.

Plaintiff

against

Defendant

> **INFORMATION SUBPOENA**
> *with Restraining Notice*
>
> *Re:*
>   *Judgment Debtor*
> *Address:*

The People of the State of New York

TO   *GREETING:*

Address:

WHEREAS, *in an action in the Civil Court of the City of New York, County of*

between

as plaintiff   **and**

as defendant
19

who are all the parties named in said action, a judgment was entered on
in favor of

judgment creditor

and against

judgment debtor
in the amount of $ *of which $*   *together with interest thereon from*
19   *remains due and unpaid; and*

WHEREAS, *the witness; resides; is regularly employed; has an office for the regular transaction of business in person;*
in   *County*

NOW, THEREFORE WE COMMAND YOU, *that you answer in writing under oath, separately and fully, each question in the questionnaire accompanying this subpoena, each answer referring to the question to which it responds; and that you return the answers together with the original of the questions within 7 days after your receipt of the questions and this subpoena.*

TAKE NOTICE *that false swearing or failure to comply with this subpoena is punishable as a contempt of court.*

RESTRAINING NOTICE

WHEREAS, *it appears that you owe a debt to the judgment debtor or are in possession or in custody of property in which the judgment debtor has an interest;*
*

TAKE NOTICE *that pursuant to subdivision (b) of Section 5222 of the Civil Practice Law and Rules, which is set forth in full herein, you are hereby forbidden to make or suffer any sale, assignment or transfer of, or any interference with, any such property or pay over or otherwise dispose of any such debt except as therein provided.*

TAKE FURTHER NOTICE *that this notice also covers all property in which the judgment debtor has an interest hereafter coming into your possession or custody, and all debts hereafter coming due from you to the judgment debtor.*

CIVIL PRACTICE LAW AND RULES

Section 5222 (b) Effect of restraint; prohibition of transfer; duration. A judgment debtor served with a restraining notice is forbidden to make or suffer any sale, assignment, transfer or interference with any property in which he has an interest, except upon direction of the sheriff or pursuant to an order of the court, until the judgment is satisfied or vacated. A restraining notice served upon a person other than the judgment debtor is effective only if, at the time of service, he owes a debt to the judgment debtor or he is in the possession or custody of property in which he knows or has reason to believe the judgment debtor has an interest, or if the judgment creditor has stated in the notice that a specified debt is owed by the person served to the judgment debtor or that the judgment debtor has an interest in specified property in the possession or custody of the person served. All property in which the judgment debtor is known or believed to have an interest then in and thereafter coming into the possession or custody of such a person, including any specified in the notice, and all debts of such a person, including any specified in the notice, then due and thereafter coming due to the judgment debtor, shall be subject to the notice. Such a person is forbidden to make or suffer any sale, assignment or transfer of, or any interference with, any such property, or pay over or otherwise dispose of any such debt, to any person other than the sheriff, except upon direction of the sheriff or pursuant to an order of the court, until the expiration of one year after the notice is served upon him, or until the judgment is satisfied or vacated, whichever event first occurs. A judgment creditor who has specified personal property or debt in a restraining notice shall be liable to the owner of the property or the person to whom the debt is owed, if other than the judgment debtor, for any damages sustained by reason of the restraint. If a garnishee served with a restraining notice withholds the payment of money belonging or owed to the judgment debtor in an amount equal to twice the amount due on the judgment, the restraining notice is not effective as to other property or money.

TAKE NOTICE *that disobedience of this Restraining Notice is punishable as a contempt of court.*

WITNESS, *Honorable*   *one of the judges of our said court,*
at the court house in the county of   *the*   *day of*   19

The name signed must be printed beneath

Attorney(s) for Judgment Creditor

Office and Post Office Address

* *Space provided if debt or property is to be specified.*

Form 13   Sample of Form for Sheriff's Sale

Sheriff's Sale!

BY VIRTUE OF AN EXECUTION ISSUED OUT OF THE____Civil____Court,____Queens____County, in favor of_____Charles Creditor_____against _____David Debtor_____, to me directed and delivered, I WILL SELL AT PUBLIC AUCTION, by____A. Smith____, auctioneer, as the law directs, FOR CASH ONLY, on the 10th day of____January____, 19 74 , at____10:____o'clock in the____fore____noon, at 182-90 Right Blvd. ____Kew Gardens, New York_____ in the County of Queens, all the right, title and interest which____John Debtor____, the judgment debtor, had on the 1st day of____January____, 1974 , or at any time thereafter, of, in and to the following property:

____1 executive desk; 1 executive chair; 1 secretary chair;

____1 secretary table; 2 steel filing cabinets; 2 cork

____bulletin boards; all carpeting; [etc.]

_____

_____

_____

_____

_____

_____

_____

_____

_____

_____

_____

JOHN Doe

Sheriff of the City of New York

____Richard Roe____ Deputy Sheriff

Queens, N. Y.,   1974

JOSEPH ATTORNEY
Attorney for Plaintiff
100-10 Concert Avenue
Jamaica, N.I.

5 57-2M-219040(64) 114

Form 13 *(continued)*

COUNTY OF QUEENS, ss.:

.... being duly sworn, says that on the................day of.., 19........., he posted copies of the within notice of sale in the following public and conspicuous places in the said County, viz.:...

One at...

One at...

One at...

One at...

One at...

One at...

Subscribed and sworn to before
  me, this...............................day
  of..............................., 19........} ....

Form 14 Sample of Income Execution

B 239—Income Execution; CPLR §5231. Civil Court. 9-1-70
6 blanks suggested; original; office copy; 2 copies each for debtor
and garnishee if officer cannot serve personally.

COPYRIGHT 1970 BY JULIUS BLUMBERG, INC., LAW BLANK PUBLISHERS
80 EXCHANGE PLACE AT BROADWAY, NEW YORK

CIVIL COURT OF THE CITY OF NEW YORK, COUNTY OF QUEENS

U. O. MEMONY COMPANY	*Index No.* 33412/73
Judgment Creditor	
against	
HENRY I. MAYO	*INCOME EXECUTION*
Judgment Debtor	
whose last known address is 220 Underhand Avenue, Flushing, New York	

The People of the State of New York

TO THE SHERIFF OR ANY MARSHAL OF THE CITY OF NEW YORK, GREETING:

In an action in the above captioned court, a judgment was duly entered in the office of the clerk of said court in favor of the Judgment Creditor and the particulars regarding said judgment are as follows:

Entry Date	Original Amount	Amount Due	Plus Interest From
3/30/73	$350.00	$350.00	3/30/73

and the Judgment Debtor is receiving or will receive from   JOINT CONSTRUCTION CO., INC.
(hereinafter referred to as the "Employer")
whose address is   150-38 68th Avenue, Flushing, Queens, New York
more than $85.00 per week, to wit $ 250.00   *to be paid in* **weekly** *amounts of* $ 250.00   *each:*

Title or Position	Bureau, Office, Dept. or Subdivision	Soc. Sec. and/or Pension No.
Office Manager	Salvage Department	011-21-3318

NOW, THEREFORE, WE COMMAND YOU, *(1)* to serve a copy of this Income Execution upon Judgment Debtor within twenty days after it is delivered to you; *(2)* if you are unable to do so, or if Judgment Debtor fails to pay the instalments pursuant to this Income Execution for a period of twenty days, you shall levy upon the monies Judgment Debtor is receiving or will receive from the Employer, by serving the Employer with a copy of this Income Execution, endorsed to indicate the extent to which paid instalments, if any, have satisfied the aforesaid judgment and *(3)* if this Income Execution remains unsatisfied, in whole or in part because you are unable to find the Employer within your jurisdiction, you shall return this Income Execution to Judgment Creditor's attorney, endorsed to indicate the extent to which paid instalments, if any, have satisfied the judgment.

DIRECTIONS TO JUDGMENT DEBTOR
YOU ARE HEREBY NOTIFIED AND COMMANDED IMMEDIATELY, to commence paying to the Sheriff or Marshal delivering a copy of this Income Execution to you, instalments amounting to 10% of any and all salary, wages or other income, including any and all overtime earnings, commissions or other irregular compensation received or hereafter to be received from your Employer and to continue paying such instalments until the judgment together with interest thereon and the fees and expenses of this Income Execution are fully paid and satisfied and if you fail to do so this Income Execution will be served upon the Employer by the Sheriff or Marshal.

DIRECTIONS TO THE EMPLOYER
YOU ARE HEREBY COMMANDED, to withhold and pay over to the Sheriff or Marshal delivering a copy of this Income Execution to you, instalments amounting to 10% of any and all salary, wages or other income, including any and all overtime earnings, commissions or other irregular compensation now or hereafter becoming due to Judgment Debtor, such amount not exceeding the maximum part of the aggregate disposable earnings subject to garnishment pursuant to Title III of the Consumer Credit Protection Act, until the aforesaid judgment together with interest thereon and the fees and expenses of this income execution are fully paid and satisfied.

Dated JAMAICA, NEW YORK
August 25, 1973

Joe Sharpe
The name signed must be printed beneath
JOE SHARPE

Attorney(s) for Judgment-creditor

Office and Post Office Address
111-20 Jamaica Avenue
Jamaica, New York   11432

Form 14 *(continued)*

Date and time execution received:

Index No.

Civil Court of the City of New York
County of

Plaintiff

against

Defendant

Income Execution

Sheriff or Marshall of the City of New York
Levy and collect as within directed

....

with interest from

besides your fees, etc.

Installments paid to..........................
(date)
have satisfied the judgment to the extent of
$. principal and
$ interest.

Attorney(s) for

....
Sheriff—Marshal

Returned to the judgment creditor or his attorney
on .... because of
(date)
inability to find garnishee in New York City.

....
Sheriff—Marshal

Index

Advertising, false, 31–32
Affidavits against debtors in military service, 21
Affirmative defenses for debtors, 12–21
Agents
 credit bureaus as, 108
 extortion committed on, 109
Alimony, 11
"Annual percentage rate" of interest, 29
Assault and battery, 11, 107
Assets (property)
 in bankruptcy, 63–65, 69–72
 of businesses, 78
 collection of, by judgment creditors, 97–104
 debtor exemptions on, 53–55
 distribution of, by assignee, 85
 distribution of, in straight bankruptcy, 64, 65, 69
 fraudulent statements about, by debtors, 93
 levies on, by sheriffs, 100
 sale of, by receivers, 103
 transfer of, for judgment creditor's benefit, 103–4
 transfer of, to assignee, 80, 82–84
 See also Community property; Real property
Assignees, 82–85
Assignments for the benefit of creditors, 80–86
Attorneys' fees, 13, 29, 36–37, 41, 70, 74, 80
Automobiles
 complaints about, 44–46
 dealers of, 29
 executions on, 100–1
Automotive Consumer Action Panels (Auto CAPS), 45–46

Baby planning parties, 35
Bailable attachment orders, 98
Bankruptcy, 61–86
 assignment for the benefit of creditors and, 82–84
 actions against debtors after, 91–94

Bankruptcy (continued)
 of corporations, under Chapter X, 77–78
 Federal laws on, see Bankruptcy Act
 fees for filing of, 73, 74
 involuntary, 74–76, 83
 petitions of, 65, 68, 71, 73, 75, 76, 78
 referees in, 71, 75–79, 91
 straight, 61–70
 trustees in, 63–69, 71, 73, 74, 78
 voluntary arrangements under Chapter XI, 76–77
 Wage earners' plan of Chapter XIII, 70–74
Bankruptcy Court, see District Courts
Bankruptcy Act, 61–62, 68–74
 Chapter X, 77–78
 Chapter XI, 76–77
 See also Wage earners' plan, Chapter XIII
Banks
 exclusion of, from involuntary bankruptcy, 74
 as holder in due course, 41
 loans from, 46–47
 nonapplication of legal interest rates to, 13
 purchase of contracts by, 27–28, 41–42, 101
 rights to insurance policies and, 55
 Truth in Lending Law regulation of interest charged by, 29
Blockbusting, 48–49
Body executions (orders of arrest), 103
Bonds filed by assignees, 84, 85
Borrowing corporations, nonapplication of legal interest rates to, 13
Burglar alarms, 33–34
Business Corporation Law of New York State, Article X, 85–86
Businesses
 bankruptcy of, 64, 76–77
 bulk transfers by, 93–94
 out-of-court settlements by, 80
 See also Corporations

171

Cancellation
 of courses of instruction, 34
 of installment contracts, 42
Certificate of Doing Business, 18
Chain (pyramid) scheme, 35–36
Chattels, 20, 70
Child Protection Act, 31
Churning by stockbrokers, 47–48
City Council of New York City, 32
Civil Law, 86
Civil Practice Law and Rules, Section
 5205 (a) of New York State,
 53–54
Class action suits, 36–37
Clerk of the court, 5
Clerk of the District Court, 71
Collection agencies, purchase of
 judgments by, 47
Collection letters, false statements
 on, 33
Common Law, 87
Common law writs, 6n
Community property, laws concern-
 ing, 85–87
Complaints to manufacturers, 44–46
Composition agreements, 79–80
 See also Out-of-court settlements
Congress, 20, 37
 bankruptcy laws of, 61
 See also Bankruptcy Act
Consideration, lack of, 19–20
Consumer Affairs, Department of, of
 New York City, 32–36
Consumer Affairs, Office of, of the
 United States, 45
Consumer Fraud Bureau of New
 York City, 35
Consumer protection, laws and agen-
 cies for, 25–37, 45–46, 112–23
Consumer Protection Act, *see* Truth
 in Lending Law
Consumer Protection Law of New
 York City (1969), 32
Consumers (buyers), 26–28, 38,
 47–48
Contempt of court, 11, 98, 100
Contractors
 collection of debts by, 105

Contractors *(continued)*
 misrepresentation of services by,
 33–34, 41
Contracts
 copies of, 3
 future service, 34
 home improvement, 25–26
 installment, 26, 28, 41–42
 lack of consideration in, 19–20
 language barrier to understanding
 of, 26
 in out-of-court settlements, 79
 as proof of purchase, 5–6
 signed under mistake or duress,
 18–19
 signing of, 3–4
 unconscionable, 25–28
 unwritten, 16–17
 voiding of, by infants, 14
Corporations
 bankruptcy of, 61, 62
 dissolution of, by stockholders, 85
 extortion committed on, 109
 filing of Certificate of Doing Business by, 18
 reorganization of, under Chapter
 X, 77–78
 purchase of judgments by, 47
 statutes concerning, 85–86
Counterclaims, 16
County clerk, 18, 84
Courts
 agreements enforceable by, 17
 Bankruptcy, *see* District Courts
 costs of, 29
 Housing, of New York City, 50
 proving fraud in, 16
 rulings on purchased judgments
 by, 47
 settlements out of, *see* Out-of-court
 settlements
 state, 92, 93
 Superior, 85
 Supreme, 85
Courses of instruction, cancellation
 of, 34
Credit after bankruptcy, 62–63, 74
Credit bureaus as agents, 108

Credit cards
  issuers of, 29
  lost, stolen, or misused, 43–44
  statutes concerning, 43
Credit charges, 28, 29
Credit unions, 29, 56
  debt pooling by, 79

Debt counsellors, 78–79
Debt pooling, 78–79
Debtor and Creditor Law of New
  York State, Article X, 93
Deceptive Practice Act of New York
  State, 31–32
Defenses, affirmative, for debtors,
  12–21, 92
Dentists, 29
Department of Commerce, 31
Department stores, 29
Deposits, 4
Disability benefits, 55
Discharge in straight bankruptcy,
  92–93
Disposable earnings, 102
District Courts
  as Bankruptcy Court, 65, 66,
    75–79, 82–85, 91, 92
  clerk of, 71, 73, 75
Domestic Relations Law, Section 52,
  of New York State, 55
Duress, contracts signed under,
  18–19

Educational Law of New York State,
  Section 524, 56
Electricians, 29
Employees
  bankrupt, 70–74
  discharge of, by employers, 102
  income executions against wages
    of, 101–2
  rights of, 33
Employers
  communication with creditors of
    employees by, 32–33
  deductions from wages of em-
    ployees made by, 71
  discharge of employees by, 102

Employers (continued)
  payment of wages by, 69, 70
Enforcement proceedings to collect
  judgments, 53
England
  Common Law of, 87
  usury laws in, 12
Eviction of members of military service, 21
Exact cost, 3
Executions
  against members of military serv-
    ice, 21
  body, 103
  debtors' property exempt from,
    53–57, 69
  income, see Income executions
  issued to sheriffs or marshals,
    100–1
  by judgment creditors, 6, 84, 100
  of purchased judgments, 47
  on salaries, 70
Exemptions
  of debtors, from executions,
    53–57, 69, 80
  homestead, 54, 56, 69, 129
  waiving of, 71
Extortion committed by judgment
  creditors, 109

Families of debtors
  extortion committed on, 109
  obligations of members of, 20
Federal Bankruptcy Act, see Bank-
  ruptcy Act
Federal Consumer Protection Act, see
  Truth in Lending Law
Finance companies
  charges of, 28
  installment plans and, 2–4
  purchase of contracts by, 27–28,
    41–42
Firemen, benefits of, 56
Flammable Products Act, 31
Food, Drug and Cosmetic Act, 31
Food plans, 27–28
Fraud, 16
  committed by debtors, 93

173

174

Judgment debtors *(continued)*
  transfer of assets of, for the benefit
    of creditors, 103–4
Judgments, 4
  collection of, 6–7, 53, 80, 93, 97–
    104
  consent, 34
  default, 5, 20
  deficiency, 4, 54
  enforcement of, by states, 6*n*
  property exempt from execution
    of, 53–57, 80
  purchase of, 47

Labor Law of New York State, Sec-
    tion 595, 56
Land, sale of, 17
Landlords
  payments to, 86
  problems with tenants of, 49–50
  language as a barrier to under-
    standing contracts, 3
  letters to automobile manufactur-
    ers, 46
Levies by sheriffs on property of
    debtors, 100
Libel, 107–8
Licenses
  loss of, 64
  of real estate brokers, 49
Liens
  of contractors, subcontractors and
    materialmen, 104
  Maritime Commission, 62
  on real property, 100
Loans, 12–13
  bank, 46–47

Mail, unsolicited merchandise sent
    through, 43
Manufacturers, complaints to, 44–46
Maritime Commission liens, 62
Marshals, 6
  collection of debtors' property by,
    53, 54
  executions issued to, 100–1
  serving of subpoenas by, 75
Mass restitution, 36

Materialmen, collection of debts by,
    104
Medicaid of New York State, 56
Meetings of creditors, 66, 77
Mental institutions, employees of, 56
Merchandise, unsolicited, 43
Merchants, 3–4
Military service
  protection of members of, 20–21,
    55, 56
  proof of membership in, 21
Mistake, contracts signed by, 18
Moratoriums in out-of-court settle-
    ments, 79
Mortgage brokers, residential, 29
Mortgages
  on automobiles, 100–1
  on community property, 86
  on real estate, 70
  stays of foreclosure on, 20
  See also Mortgage brokers
Motor Vehicles Retail Installment
    Sales Act of New York, 19
Mutuality of agreement, 18
Myerson, Bess, 33

National Service Life Insurance poli-
    cies, 56
National Tenant Information Service,
    50
Necessities, 14, 91
Negligence, 31, 103
"Noticed for trial," 5

Orders
  of arrest, 103
  bailable attachment, 98
  installment payment, 102
  restraining, 64, 65, 99–100
  served on judgment debtors and
    witnesses, 98
Out-of-court settlements, 77, 79–80
  by businesses, 80
  contracts in, 79
  moratoriums in, 79

Penal Law of New York State, 109
Pensions, 55

175